'Hang in there. It is astonishing how short a time it can take for very wonderful things to happen.'

Frances Hodgson Burnett

Jen Chillingsworth

LIVE GREEN

52 steps for a more
sustainable life

Illustrations by Amelia Flower

WITHDRAWN

Hardie Grant

QUADRILLE

Publishing Director Sarah Lavelle
Junior Commissioning Editor Harriet Butt
Senior Designer Gemma Hayden
Illustrator Amelia Flower
Production Director Vincent Smith
Production Controller Nikolaus Ginelli

Published in 2019 by Quadrille,
an imprint of Hardie Grant Publishing

Quadrille
52–54 Southwark Street
London SE1 1UN
quadrille.com

Cataloguing in Publication Data: a catalogue
record for this book is available from the
British Library.

Text © Jen Chillingsworth 2019
Illustrations © Amelia Flower 2019
Design and layout © Quadrille 2019

Reprinted in 2019 (three times)
10 9 8 7 6 5 4

ISBN 978 1 78713 319 8

Printed in China

Contents

Introduction

Many of us are already doing what we can to adopt a greener lifestyle. We recycle, try to reduce our waste and plastics, choose organic food when we go grocery shopping, eat less meat and opt for environmentally-friendly cleaning products. And yet we often wish we were doing even more as we see news reports and nature programmes on television depicting the terrifying and long-lasting damage done to our planet by humankind. We try to make changes that we think will work for us and for the planet, and when the result is not as we might have wished, we're left dealing with environmental guilt and a sense of failure. I've been there and speak from experience.

When my son was young, I was working in a busy arts management job and constantly felt anxious and frustrated. Racing to get my son to school, enduring a stressful commute to work and then sitting in meetings with toxic people made me dread every single day. I knew I wasn't happy and that my way of coping with this sense of dissatisfaction and unease was to buy lots of things – clothes, magazines, expensive skincare lotions, DVDs, chocolates, bottles and bottles of wine. Essentially, I loved to consume. The delivery man who brought parcels to my door visited so often that I saw him more than my best friends. When my husband had to make a career change due to redundancy, his new job in healthcare made childcare even harder for us as we would both be working late nights. We made the joint decision that I'd leave my stressful job and try to find something more suited to our family's lifestyle.

At home I believed that I was doing what I could to help the environment. I'd buy recycled

products, organic milk and greener cleaning products. We separated our household rubbish and recycling, and took what wasn't collected by our local council to the recycling centre. We never left lights on in empty rooms or let the water run as we brushed our teeth. Any leftovers from dinner were eaten up for lunch the next day. I believed we were doing what we could, but at that time I never once thought about the sheer number of plastic bags we used doing our grocery shop, I didn't consider the single-use bottles and cartons for my son's packed lunches a problem as I could simply pop them in the recycling bin, and I ignored the fact that I possessed an extensive collection of laundry liquid dosing caps which continued to grow as I got a new one every time I bought the product.

I was lucky enough to find a part-time job in a market garden run by a local family only ten minutes from our home, and this proved to be a turning point. Being outdoors in the sunshine on a glorious

summer's day (as well as on the hard, wet, dark days of winter), I learned to grow fruits, vegetables and other plants, to understand when seeds needed to be sowed so they would be ready at the right time of year, and to harvest crops properly. These were great new skills to master, but it also taught me how much physical effort goes into creating the food on our plates and how important nature is to our wellbeing. Working outside all day left me appreciating how good it was to feel the sun on my face, indulging in the scent of fresh herbs that I'd grown from cuttings and watching the bees forage for nectar on the perennials in the plant nursery. I would return home covered in mud, utterly exhausted yet happier than I had been in a long time.

The market garden became the place where I learned more about how to look after the land from an environmental point of view. We didn't spray crops with pesticides and we'd regularly discover a caterpillar nestling in amongst the cabbage leaves. Weeds would spring up in the field surrounding the crops, and what originally had been neat rows of cauliflowers, kale and squashes would vanish from view. Time spent harvesting often meant getting an arm or leg covered in painful nettle stings, but it was always worth it. After a quick rinse in water, those vegetables, freshly picked from the field, had real flavour and tasted amazing.

My change of career gave me a happier way of working, but it also brought with it a significant drop in income, and with less money coming in I really needed to curb my spending habits. In many ways life had become easier as I only worked during my son's school terms and didn't have to pay for childcare. My job was within walking distance of home and our fuel costs were hugely reduced. My previous income had been three times what I was making at the market garden, meaning we were now in the position of not being able to afford luxury items and holidays abroad were out of the question. Yet the first school

summer holiday I spent at home with my son provided me with some of my happiest memories and I know that they had a huge impact on how I choose to live my life now. We roamed around the woods and countryside, observing our local wildlife, flora and trees and foraging for blackberries and bilberries on the moors. We camped in sand dunes, listened to the waves lap the beach and gazed in awe at the constellations in the night sky. Our natural world was incredible. I started to appreciate a much simpler way of living and to document our family adventures and lifestyle changes on my blog.

From my experience of living a slower, simpler life came a greater understanding of our impact on future generations. I wanted to teach my son how to live with more intention – less buying, more doing, less wanting, more enjoying what we already had. As a family we were embracing simple living and when we did have to buy something, we tried to make considered purchases that dovetailed with our new values and looked at ways we could make both our home and lifestyle greener. From walking to the supermarket and reducing food waste, to switching to 'bags for life' and buying vintage clothing – these were all relatively easy ways for us to help the environment. Even though we made these changes I still felt we had a long way to go. Reading books on the environment, watching documentaries and looking at websites dedicated to making a difference left me feeling completely overwhelmed, conflicted and guilty that I wasn't doing enough.

I found that many books and articles suggested changes that were not practical or accessible to us. From that point on I started to realise that I could choose to do things simply and slowly, and make small changes that would be achievable for us and become part of everyday living. Over the course of a year, we followed this path and although a couple of ideas turned out to be complete disasters, the rest have made our home run much

more smoothly, made our lifestyle easier and many have saved us money, too.

This book is a collection of the changes we've made in our home and lifestyle and I hope you'll find them helpful. My tips are for anyone and everyone, no matter where you live or what job you do. Many are simply about modifying habits so they become part of our daily lives. These are achievable, useful and practical ideas and I truly believe that small steps lead to big changes.

We are all at different places and stages in our lives, yet we are all in this together to help look after our beautiful planet.

LIVE SIMPLY.
LIVE GREEN.

LIVE WITH MORE INTENTION
less buying, more doing,
less wanting, more enjoying

Green Home
& Garden

'Home is the nicest word there is.'
Laura Ingalls Wilder

Green home & garden

I truly believe that our homes should not only provide us with shelter, but also bring us joy. No matter how big or small it is, our home is where we nurture our children, it offers us a place of retreat after a stressful day, and provides us with sanctuary throughout the darkness of winter.

We spend many hours in our homes, so it's important to take a more considered approach to what we bring into them. From the paint on the wall and the bedlinen we sleep in, to the energy we consume – it all has an impact on our wellbeing and the wider environment.

Decluttering

We all have too much stuff that we don't need, like or use anymore. I had cupboards and drawers that wouldn't close because they had too much forgotten clutter pushed into them – you probably have some of those too! Decluttering our homes helps us in so many ways: creating a calmer environment; less searching for misplaced items; and a reduction in the amount of cleaning and dusting (which is always welcome!).

Many of us think that the solution to sorting out all our belongings is to buy more storage containers, whereas the answer is we simply have too much stuff! Getting rid of junk, switching to paperless options for household admin and donating things we don't need anymore all help us to become greener in our homes.

Set aside an amount of time – say 30 minutes – and set a timer on your phone. Take one room, cupboard or drawer and during that time get rid of the things you no longer use or want to keep. Divide these into groups – one pile of rubbish to be discarded, one pile to be donated to charity/given to friends or family and, if you want to sell some items, then a pile for those too. A good question to ask yourself as you go through your belongings is when was the last time I used this? If it's more than a year ago, then let it go.

IN THE BEDROOM

Donate any used, clean bedding and blankets to a local homeless shelter or animal rescue. Throw out single socks or items that have shrunk in the wash, or use them for cleaning rags. Donate clothes to the charity shop or thrift store or arrange a clothes swap party with friends (see page 125).

IN THE BATHROOM

Clear out any out-of-date medicines and return them to the pharmacy rather than flushing them down the toilet where they can enter the water supply. Many of us receive beauty gift packs at Christmas that we never use so donate them to charity.

IN THE LIVING ROOM

Clear out magazine and newspaper piles for recycling. Cancel subscriptions – most magazines have paperless online versions. Gather CDs and DVDs that you never watch anymore and either sell or donate them. Do the same with any books you won't read again – many libraries accept donated books if they are in good condition, benefitting your community too. Either give any homewares that you no longer want or have use for to charity, or sell them at a car boot or yard sale. Board games or jigsaws can be donated to playgroups, after-school clubs, the children's ward at the local hospital or a care home for the elderly.

IN THE KITCHEN

Clear out that kitchen drawer full of rubbish (everyone has one!). Recycle takeout menus and junk mail. Clear out out-of-date food packets and cleaning supplies that linger at the back of cupboards.

Kitchenware is always popular at car boot and yard sales, so take along pans, casserole dishes and storage containers and they will always be some of the first things to go. Look at how many mugs or plates you have – we are a small family of three, yet we had over twenty mugs! Donate or sell – either way you are passing them on to someone who needs them.

Decluttering tips

» *Inherited/keepsakes* This might be an item you don't really use, like or need, but you keep it all the same. You do this because you feel like you should, rather than focusing on what the item really means to you. I kept my wedding dress for years after I got married, even though I was never going to wear it again and it wouldn't fit me anymore. I felt like I should hold on to it as it marked a significant moment in my life, yet my memories of the day were more important to me than the actual dress, so I eventually donated it to charity. Whether it's an inherited piece of furniture, a box of baby clothes or a gift from a loved one, the key to letting go of these items is asking yourself what they really mean to you. If you have a strong emotional attachment to a physical item then keep it, if not, think about letting it go.

» *Kids mementoes* As parents it's difficult to let go of items our kids have made, so we pop them in cupboards and drawers, often forgetting about them. We also think our kids might want to have these precious mementoes when they grow up, but the reality is, they probably won't want to take them with them. Instead of keeping every piece of artwork, twig or handmade card, choose a couple that are the most important to you. Before you get rid of the other things, take photographs or scan artwork into your computer. Use them to compile a scrapbook of memories that you can all look at together in the future.

Green decorating

You've probably heard about VOCs (volatile organic compounds) and how they can cause a variety of health problems. VOCs are emitted as gases from solids or liquids and are widely used in paint, varnish and wax. With paint, VOCs are released during the drying process and they can remain toxic for months or even years after application. Some of them have carcinogenic properties and they also cause harm to the environment, which is why their use in paint is strictly controlled by legislation. Most brands now offer low-VOC paints for indoor projects, but they often still contain other nasties like ammonia, formaldehyde and acrylic softeners – all major sources of indoor air pollution.

continued »

Switch to green alternatives:

PAINT FOR WALLS

Many eco paints are virtually free from VOCs, are breathable and are great for rooms like kitchens and bathrooms as they are formulated to help reduce condensation, mould and mildew. However, not all are washable, so in time you will probably have to touch up areas that get dirty. Switching to a more environmentally friendly paint may help alleviate symptoms for allergy or asthma sufferers too. I like to use clay paint, which you can buy already made up or as a powder. Casein paint is also a good choice, but it is made from milk protein and therefore not suitable for vegans.

PAINT FOR INTERIOR WOODWORK

Choose environmentally friendly water-based gloss or eggshell. It's best to avoid oil-based varieties, although some brands are now introducing paints made with vegetable oils.

WAX/VARNISH

For flooring and woodwork, look for non-toxic, natural water-based products. Waxes are usually made with beeswax, but plant-based waxes are also available if you are vegan.

FURNITURE PAINT

Opt for paints that are chalk- or mineral-based. The best brands are virtually free from VOCs and contain no formaldehyde or ammonia. They offer good coverage, require little preparation before painting and are washable, too.

PAINTING IN A NURSERY

If you are decorating a nursery, look for paints that conform to the 'Toy Paint Regulations' (or similar legislation in your own country) as not all paints are safe to use on walls or furniture. Babies and toddlers love to chew things, so it's reassuring to know that they won't come to any harm if they nibble the bars on their crib! Do some research before you buy to make sure that all the nasties have been removed. Most eco brands produce paint that is safe for babies and young children.

LEFTOVER PAINT

Check with your local council for recycling options or look online to donate to charity organizations who can reuse or resell your leftovers.

WALLPAPER

Opt for brands that make wallpaper from Forest Stewardship Council (FSC) certified paper. This means the trees used are managed responsibly, and for every tree felled, more are planted. Alternatively, choose recycled wallpaper as this creates less waste and no trees are felled in the process. There are lots of options available now for patterns printed with non-toxic water-based inks and it's easy to source great vintage wallpaper too. Look for paste or adhesive that is free from acrylics, solvents and fungicides.

Energy efficiency

When it comes to energy in the home, it's easy to make small changes that can add up to big results for the environment and for our finances. Most of these ideas are simply about making a shift in our habits. We've made all the changes listed below in our home and have found our bills have reduced as well as keeping us toasty warm throughout the colder months.

SWITCH TO A GREEN ENERGY SUPPLIER

Changing to a renewable energy supplier has never been easier and it's worth doing if it's going to save you money and you want to cut your carbon footprint. Renewables reduce the production of carbon dioxide and the release of other greenhouse gases into the atmosphere, reduce our dependence on oil and coal, and make use of local resources. Search online for the best deal and look for companies that provide 100% renewable electricity.

HEATING

Reduce the temperature on your thermostat by one degree and you'll find a significant reduction in your bill, while barely noticing the difference. If you have thermostats on your radiators, set the temperature for each room that requires heating.

GET A SMART METER

These show you exactly how much energy you are using and how much it costs. Seeing the numbers creep up on the meter makes you think more about any energy you are wasting, encouraging you to make positive changes where you can.

TELEVISION

Did you know that the larger the television you have, the more electricity it uses? Choosing a smaller screen will save you money and energy. Also, don't forget to turn it off when you leave the room and don't leave it on standby as it's still drawing power.

RADIATOR FOIL

My Grandpa used to take large sheets of cardboard, wrap them in foil and pop them behind his radiators. As a child I thought this was mad as I didn't understand their purpose! But it's a simple and effective way to prevent heat escaping from your home. The sheet of foil reflects the heat and bounces it back in to the room rather than it escaping through the walls of your home. Using radiator foil can heat your room up much quicker and it can cut heat loss by 50%. Rather than using kitchen foil, opt for sheets of radiator foil that you can buy at the hardware store. There are magnetic versions available which make it even easier to fit.

DRAUGHT EXCLUDERS

We lose a lot of heat from gaps under doors and windows. Use a self-adhesive foam or rubber draught seal on small gaps around window frames and look for brush-type seals for use on letterboxes. For larger gaps around doors, make your own excluder from old tights/pantyhose. Cut one leg off a pair of tights and either fill it with stuffing available from craft shops or by shredding up other old tights. Tie the ends together. If you want something prettier, find some nice fabric and sew your own.

COOKING

Keep the lids on saucepans to help food cook quicker, put frozen dishes in the fridge overnight rather than defrosting using a microwave, fill the kettle or a pan with onlythe amount of water you need, and try not to use the oven to only cook one thing.

Choosing vintage for your home

Buying flat-pack furniture is the way many of us furnish our homes as it's both affordable, adaptable and accessible. Sadly, it's not always built to last and it often gets sent to landfill when it can't be repaired, so it's a good idea to be more mindful when selecting a new piece of furniture. Buying less and looking for alternatives are good ways to start. I'm a big advocate of shopping for vintage items for my home and I've stumbled upon some great pieces in local charity shops, thrift stores, flea markets and vintage fairs. I love the fact that you can repurpose an item, give it a new home and find something truly unique.

If you are trying to source furniture from a certain era, then it's a good idea to research all the makers from that period. Some designers sell for more money than others as they are currently on trend, yet pieces in a similar style from a different maker can be just as good.

I'd been searching for some mid-century dining chairs for years and they can command a high price on auction websites. Eventually I got super lucky, bagging two in a charity shop and one in a tiny vintage store for a fraction of what I would have paid online. The single chair had been painted a lurid shade of pink and decorated with purple butterfly stencilling, so I got it for a few pounds as it needed a lot of work to restore it. After a few hours of sanding and a couple of coats of wax, it was good as new.

When visiting fairs or salvage yards, I find it useful to make a note on my phone as a reminder of what I'm searching for. There is often so much choice that it can be overwhelming and it's good to go prepared. Talk to the traders and don't be afraid to haggle by asking for a price reduction. You may feel embarrassed at first, but dealers are used to it. Check items thoroughly before you buy to ensure they are sound and factor in any repair costs as part of the price. Take a tape measure and a list of measurements with you to make sure anything you want to buy will fit your space at home. And don't forget to make sure that you can physically get it home or that delivery can be arranged, and that it will fit through the front door or up the stairs.

Search online for local vintage stores and salvage yards and then visit them regularly. Getting to know dealers is an excellent way of finding what you are looking for as they can source items for you too.

KEEP IT SIMPLE AT FIRST

Buy artwork, textiles or simple storage, i.e. items that can easily be brought into your home. Look for items that can be repurposed too – enamel buckets make great planters for house or garden plants and carboy bottles from France make wonderful vases and terrariums. Lighting or electricals that need rewiring should be taken to an electrician, so they can be made safe before use.

Repurposing and upcycling

Repurposing or upcycling an existing piece of furniture can give it a new lease of life and prevent it from being sent to landfill. Even flat-pack furniture can be transformed into a unique piece for your home by making some simple changes.

PAINT IT

We were really taken with a closet we saw in a more expensive high-street store, but it was well out of our price range. Instead, we opted to buy a similar looking yet cheaper flat-pack one and upcycle it with paint. A couple of coats later, the cheaper closet looked as good as the more expensive one. Painting new and vintage furniture takes a little work but it's worth the effort. Choose mineral or chalk paint for furniture as they are both non-toxic and low in VOCs (see page 19).

Here are some other ideas for repurposing or upcycling in the home and garden:

IN THE HOME

» Use an old sweater to upholster a bench or a footstool. Spread the sweater flat on the floor and turn the piece of furniture upside down on top of the sweater. Wrap it around the bench/footstool and then staple the fabric tightly underneath. Trim the excess.

» Turn old fruit and wine crates into shelving for books or crockery, or turn them on their end for a great bedside table. Give them a quick lick of paint – either chalk or mineral-based paint is perfect for use on furniture.

» Take an old picture frame and make your own original art for inside it. Head out on a foraging walk to pick some wildflowers from the woods or hedgerows, but be sure to forage responsibly

and not remove any endangered species. Alternatively, pick some flowers and herbs from the garden. Make sure they are dry before pressing them between some sheets of good-quality blotting paper. Cover the sheets with a heavy weight – cookery books are ideal for this – and leave for a week. Arrange your pressed flowers against a sheet of white or black card, then pop it in the frame.

» An old vintage bookcase or display cabinet looks great painted with either mineral or chalk paint and then lined with wallpaper offcuts or floral wrapping paper.

IN THE GARDEN

» Turn pieces of enamelware into planters. Mugs, bowls, storage jars and teapots look great planted up with herbs. Drill a couple of holes in the bottom of the enamelware and add a small handful of gravel to help with drainage.

» Use old woollen sweaters to line hanging baskets or containers. These have great moisture-retaining qualities, particularly during hot weather when container plants need extra water. Afterwards, the sweater can go in the compost heap.

» Old chairs can also be reinvented as planters. Remove the seat and replace with a bucket or a plant pot that fits in the gap without falling through. These look wonderful planted up with succulents.

Natural plant fibres in the home

One of the best ways we can be greener in our homes is to make a switch from manmade fibres to natural ones. Stores are full of homeware products made from synthetic materials, from cushions and curtains to blankets and bedlinen. Manmade fibres are far cheaper and easier to produce than natural fibres, but they are derived from petrochemicals, use a lot of energy during the manufacturing process, are not biodegradable and ultimately end up in landfill. Choosing natural fibres helps to support employment and the economies of developing nations as they are mostly grown and harvested there. Natural plant fibres are biodegradable, compostable and easily recyclable, too.

I've been gradually replacing synthetic items like curtains, bedding and cushions with ones made from all-natural fibres. Getting into a bed made with linen sheets and pillowcases for the first time is utter bliss and you'll never want to sleep in anything else, I promise!

Green alternatives

ORGANIC COTTON

Most cotton crops are heavily sprayed with pesticides and herbicides. These harmful chemicals leach into the soil and enter rivers and groundwater, causing pollution and long-term health problems for the surrounding communities.

Switching to organically farmed cotton helps the environment as it encourages biodiversity, uses far less water and is not intensively sprayed, if at all, with pesticides.

Terry towels for the bathroom, dish towels, bedlinen and blankets made from organic cotton can all be easily found in stores or online.

LINEN

This is made from the flax plant. The whole plant is harvested and used for food and fabric so it's zero waste too. While growing, it requires far less water than cotton and no chemical fertilizers. Linen resists sunlight and is a great insulator so it's the perfect fabric for curtains. It won't pill, is long lasting and gets softer with age. It also keeps you cool in summer and warm in winter.

Choose bedlinen, towels and cushion covers in linen, but look for brands that use European flax. This guarantees it's grown by farmers who respect the environment and have adopted a zero irrigation, zero GMO and zero-waste policy.

SISAL

Sisal fibre is obtained from the leaves of the agave plant. It's spun into yarn which is then used to make rugs. Sisal is durable and stronger than jute or coir, which are also often used to make rugs or carpets.

HEMP

Hemp is fast growing, requires no pesticides, helps to remove pesticides from the soil and is drought resistant. It is anti-bacterial, durable and completely biodegradable. You can buy hemp towels, tablecloths, cushion covers and shower curtains online.

DYES

Textiles made from natural fibres are often dyed and treated with synthetic ingredients, so wherever possible try to buy textiles that have been coloured with dyes made from plant-based ingredients. Or opt for natural textiles like linen and hemp and have a go at making your own dyes from avocado skins, onions, roses, cherries, strawberries and lavender. There are plenty of great online tutorials that show you how to do this.

Bring the outside in

I love filling my home with plants. They bring me joy, happiness, colour on the dullest of days and most importantly of all, they help to purify the air in my home.

In 1989, NASA conducted research on ways to keep the air in the space station clean. They discovered that certain houseplants significantly eliminated toxins such as benzene, formaldehyde and trichloroethylene from the air. These toxins are commonly found in our homes in paint, cleaning products, carpets and plastics. Many can cause side effects such as headaches, nausea, dizziness and respiratory problems when exposed to them long-term. Although the study was done nearly 30 years ago, the results still stand and bringing plants into your home or workplace means you benefit by breathing in cleaner, healthier air.

These are some of the best houseplants to help clean the air, plus a few pointers for looking after them. Throughout the growing season, feed them with a liquid seaweed fertilizer or an organic plant food. Be mindful if you have a pet as cats and dogs can nibble plants that are toxic. Pop them somewhere out of harm's way if you want to ensure your furry friends stay safe.

SNAKE PLANT/MOTHER-IN-LAW'S TONGUE
Sansevieria trifasciata
Prefers bright light, but can take some shade too. Water in spring and summer, thoroughly wetting the soil. Allow the top few centimetres/inch to dry out between each watering. Water sparingly in autumn and winter.

SPIDER PLANT
Chlorophytum comosum
Likes bright, indirect light. Water well in spring and summer, sparingly in autumn and winter. It does grow very quickly, so needs to be re-potted each spring. Great for bedrooms and it's been known to remove 90% of toxins from the air in under two days.

PEACE LILY *Spathiphyllum*
Likes indirect sunlight and shade. Especially good in bathrooms where it thrives in humid conditions, but equally happy elsewhere if it gets a regular misting with water. Take care not to overwater. It's a great choice for office environments as it can tolerate fluorescent lighting.

IVY *Hedera*
Likes indirect sunlight and partial shade. Mist it well in the summer. Ivy is ideal in a home where someone smokes as it soaks up second hand carcinogens.

WEEPING FIG *Ficus benjamina*
Likes a bright room and even enjoys a little direct sun first thing in the morning. Keep moist throughout spring and summer but don't let it sit in water as it may suffer from root rot. It's been found to be the best plant for removing formaldehyde released from carpets and furniture.

BOSTON FERN
Nephrolepis exaltata
Likes indirect sunlight and loves humidity, so it's perfect for steamy bathrooms. Keep the soil moist in spring and summer but reduce watering in autumn and winter.

Scenting the home naturally

We like our homes to smell welcoming, but this can mean masking the aromas of cooking or the whiff of pets. Many of us reach for air freshener sprays, plug-ins or scented candles, yet they are full of chemicals that harm the environment and release toxins into the air in our home. Aim to open your windows once a day to let some fresh air in and help to counteract indoor air pollution.

Choosing candles

Most scented candles are made from paraffin wax (also known as mineral wax). A petroleum waste product, paraffin is bleached, synthetically coloured and fragranced to make a scented candle. When it's burning, the fumes released are comparable with those from a diesel engine and are especially harmful to anyone who suffers with asthma and other respiratory problems. Paraffin wax candles also produce a lot of smoke and can leave soot residue on the walls. Instead, choose eco-friendly candles made with cotton wicks and scented with essential oils.

» *Beeswax* Gives off a delicate honey scent and is a natural air purifier. Non-allergenic, non-toxic and smoke free.

» *Soy* Non-toxic and suitable for vegans. Look for responsibly sourced and non-GMO soy products.

» *Rapeseed (Canola)* Non-toxic and suitable for vegans. Look for responsibly sourced and non-GMO rapeseed products. In the UK and EU this is by far the best choice as it has the lowest carbon footprint.

» *Coconut* Non-toxic, burns clean and slow. Sustainable and organic but expensive.

It's not only scented candles made with paraffin wax – unscented dinner candles, tealights, etc. all release toxins, so look for natural alternatives if you use them. Don't forget you can recycle the glass jars that some candles come in.

Other natural alternatives

ESSENTIAL OILS AND A DIFFUSER

Switch from a plug-in air freshener to a steam diffuser. They gently release essential oils into the air and are especially good in the bedroom used with lavender oil to help you sleep better.

NATURAL AIR FRESHENER

Add bicarbonate of soda (baking soda) to a depth of 3 – 4cm (1½in) to a glass jar, then sprinkle in a few drops of your favourite essential oil. Punch a couple of holes in the jar lid and screw it on. Once the smell begins to fade, simply add a few more drops of oil.

FRESH FLOWERS

Avoid buying flowers from the supermarket as they all come wrapped in plastic. Look to your local florist instead and choose seasonal flowers that are locally sourced rather than imported from overseas. As soon as you walk through the door you will be hit with the intoxicating scent of fresh flowers and foliage. I love to buy big bunches of eucalyptus as the smell is incredible and lasts for ages. If you choose flowers that not only smell great but can be dried too, then you have a bouquet that lasts for ever.

HERBS

Add a pot of fresh thyme or rosemary to the kitchen windowsill. Gently squeeze the leaves to release more of their scent. Hang up bunches of herbs to dry in the kitchen, too – sage, bay leaves, oregano, mint, etc.

Plant a tree or hedge

Air pollution is a major cause of death and disease around the world. The World Health Organization (WHO) states that air pollution claims seven million lives a year and that both short- and long-term exposure to pollutants can cause respiratory infections and reduced lung function. It's sadly getting worse in busy urban areas and we need to act now to help our future generations. One of the simplest ways to improve air quality in your own neighbourhood is plant a tree or a hedge. Both have been proven to significantly reduce air pollution.

Trees

Single trees in urban areas have been found to be far more beneficial at collecting harmful particles than those in a woodland area. Environmental scientists studied native trees in the UK and their abilities to absorb and reduce air pollution. From their findings they compiled a list of trees rated from best to worst in dealing with the effects of pollution. Known as the Urban Tree Air Quality Score (UTAQS), these were some of the highest rated trees in the UK:

FOR MEDIUM TO LARGE GARDENS

» Cherry Laurel *Prunus laurocerasus* vigorous large, evergreen shrub

» Field Maple *Acer campestre* medium size, deciduous tree

» Lawson's Cypress *Chamaecyparis lawsoniana* medium size, evergreen tree

» Norway Maple *Acer platanoides* vigorous large, deciduous tree

» Silver Birch *Betula pendula* medium size, deciduous tree

FOR SMALLER GARDENS & CONTAINERS

» Apple *Malus* Choose an apple tree. These are grafted onto different rootstock sizes, so chat with your nursery or garden centre to make sure you get the right one. You can also find larger rootstock sizes if you have the room for it. Be mindful that the birds like the fruit too, so pop a net over them when they are fruiting. For containers choose an M27 rootstock or for smaller urban gardens, an MM106 rootstock.

Hedging

Planting low hedges in urban areas can help to reduce the impact of pollution as they are closer to the level of vehicle exhaust fumes and can absorb the particles before they have the chance to disperse into the air.

FORMAL HEDGING

Leylandii and yews rate highly at trapping particles because their small needle-type leaves have the greatest surface area. They are both evergreen and good for screening.

Leylandii needs pruning two to three times a year otherwise it can grow out of control, whereas yews only need pruning once a year in early autumn. Privet hedging is also known for its pollution-busting properties. It's a fast-growing semi-evergreen that flowers in the summer and provides the birds with berries over the winter. It needs to be pruned twice a year.

INFORMAL, NATURAL HEDGING

If you are happy to let your hedge grow a little wilder, then opt for a selection of native plants. These provide homes for birds, insects and small mammals. Choose beech *Fagus sylvatica*, blackthorn *Prunus spinosa*, hawthorn *Crataegus* and holly *Ilex*. And an added benefit of planting a blackthorn is it produces sloes, perfect for making your own gin (see page 95)!

ONE OF THE SIMPLEST WAYS TO IMPROVE AIR QUALITY IN YOUR OWN NEIGHBOURHOOD IS TO PLANT A TREE OR A HEDGE.

Planting for bees

The bee population is struggling and in rapid decline, yet bees play a vital role in our food production. Most fruit and vegetables rely on bees through pollination – they transfer pollen between flowering plants, which helps plants to grow, breed and produce crops.

The number of bees has dwindled due to loss of habitat, pesticides, invasive species, farming practices and the effects of climate change. More than ever before, bees need our help. The good news is that we can do this in our own gardens.

LET THE GRASS GROW

Embrace the clover, daisies and dandelions as bees love them. Consider converting your lawn to a wildflower meadow or sowing an empty flower bed with wildflower seeds, which will give you a stunning summertime display as well as benefitting the bees.

BEST PLANTS FOR BEES

Whether you have a balcony, a windowbox or a large garden, select plants that benefit our pollinators. As some bees forage all year round, choose a range of plants that flower in each season.

Spring

» *Alpines*: arabis, aubreta, heathers, primroses

» *Climbers:* wisteria

» *Fruit bushes/trees:* apple, pear, plum

» *Shrubs:* berberis, broom, ceanothus, lilac, ribes

Summer

» *Alpines*: helianthemum, sedum

» *Herbs*: borage, chamomile, chives, hyssop, summer savory, thyme

» *Climbers:* honeysuckle, jasmine, passionflower

continued »

» *Fruit bushes/trees:* blackcurrants, blueberries, raspberries, redcurrants, strawberries

» *Perennials:* achillea, astrantia, echinacea, echinops, foxgloves, rudbeckia, salvia, scabious

» *Shrubs:* buddleja, escallonia, lavender, weigela

» *Vegetables:* broad beans (fava beans), courgettes (zucchini), runner beans, summer squashes

Autumn

» *Perennials:* dahlias, wallflowers
» *Shrubs:* abelia, fatsia
» *Vegetables:* pumpkins, squashes

Winter

» *Herbs:* rosemary
» *Shrubs:* daphne, hellebores, mahonia, skimmia

AVOID PESTICIDES

Choose an organic method to spray unwanted pests like aphids, or mites, as commercial products can be harmful to bees and other pollinators. I use a homemade spray of castile soap and water. Fill a 1-litre (35-oz) spray bottle with water and add two teaspoons of liquid castile soap (see page 54). Spray on the leaves first thing in the morning or early evening.

PROVIDE BEES WITH WATER

Bees need water to survive and honeybees use it to cool the hive in hot weather. To make your garden or balcony more bee friendly, simply fill a tray or shallow dish with water (preferably rainwater). Put a couple of large stones in the tray or dish so bees can rest easily and safely as they drink.

GIVE THEM A HOME

Unlike honeybees that live in a hive, solitary bees like to take up residence in gardens or sheds. You can buy ready-made bug and bee houses online, but I like to make my own and it's a great project to do with kids.

How to make a bee house

YOU WILL NEED

» One old, clean 2-litre
  (70-oz) plastic bottle

» Bamboo canes (different
  widths are best, so the holes
  vary in size)

» Saw or secateurs (pruning
  shears)

1 Cut the top off the old plastic bottle.

2 Cut the bamboo canes to the same length as the depth
of the bottle.

3 Pack the bamboo canes tightly into the bottle. Place in
a sunny, dry, sheltered spot, 1m (3ft) above the ground.

Eco
Household

'The true secret of happiness lies in taking a genuine interest in all the details of daily life.'

William Morris

Eco household

A few years ago, I found myself in the hospital emergency department after suffering an extreme allergic reaction to a cleaning product. I'd been scrubbing tiles in my bathroom with a bleach-based solution and although I'd ventilated the room well, it had still managed to overwhelm my system. My face, arms and hands had swollen to twice their normal size, and my skin was itchy and covered in a rash. Thankfully it hadn't affected my breathing, but I felt awful and I vowed not to let it happen again.

This experience made me look more closely at cleaning products and the harm they can do to our wellbeing and to the environment. I started making some simple changes, switching to environmentally friendly versions of multi-surface sprays and washing powders, avoiding anything that contains bleach.

Our supermarket shelves are jam packed with cleaning supplies and there is a different product available for every conceivable household task. From antibacterial sprays, drain cleaners, fridge deodorizers, granite and marble countertop sprays, stainless steel polishes to shower sprays, we are encouraged to buy a separate bottle for each appliance or item of hardware. Yet most of these products are made from toxic chemicals that have the potential to damage our health, as well as contribute to the increasing problem of plastics consumption.

Many of us choose a different path by buying and using more natural products to clean our homes and this is a step in the right direction. However, if you want to do a little more than that, over the next few pages you'll find plenty of hints and tips for small changes that can make a difference.

Recycling household waste

My goal for this year has been to reduce the amount of household waste we produce.

I've been much more aware of checking all packaging to see if it can be recycled at the kerbside, as well as choosing alternatives when it can't be recycled at all. Our local authority provides us with green waste bags which are collected monthly and on average we used to fill four of them, but I've now managed to get this down to two.

Every local authority collects and sorts waste differently and if you are unsure of what you can recycle check your local council website where you'll find the most up-to-date information. The online site TerraCycle is on a mission to recycle the non-recyclable and offers a wide selection of free programmes for schools, offices and in the home. They run programmes worldwide and work alongside big companies to help reduce the impact they have on the planet.

Many local authorities will pick up plastics, paper, cardboard, metal cans and glass from the kerbside, but most won't collect plastic wrappers for recycling. Certain types of plastic bags can be taken to large supermarkets where they have special collection bins. Look out for the symbol on packaging that says 'recycle with carrier bags at larger stores' and double check if your supermarket has one of these bins before you take them.

PLASTICS TO RECYCLE

All of these items can be taken to your local supermarket to be recycled:

» Plastic shopping bags, carrier bags, produce bags.

» Bread bags. Remove the plastic tag first and shake out any crumbs.

» Cereal packets. The clear bags that contain the cereal inside the recyclable cardboard packaging.

» Frozen vegetable/chip packets, but make sure you give anything greasy a wipe first.

» Toilet roll/paper towel wrappers.

» Magazine wrappers. If you subscribe to a magazine or newspaper you can recycle the packaging it is delivered in.

» Plastic wrap from multipack cans/bottles.

» Thin plastic bags used for loose fruit and vegetables at the supermarket.

OTHER RECYCLABLES
» Wine corks. If the cork isn't made from plastic or been painted, it can go in the recycling bin or be composted.

» Pet food. If you have a food caddy in the kitchen, any rejected dog or cat food can be added to human food scraps.

» Takeaway pizza boxes. Tear off any greasy parts of the box and put them in the bin. If the rest of the cardboard is clean, it can be put in the recycling bin. Alternatively, you can break up the entire box and put it in the compost bin.

WHAT NOT TO RECYCLE AT HOME
» Crisp packets. Although they look like foil inside, crisp packets are made from a metalized plastic that is not currently recyclable.

» Paper towels/tissues. If soiled they cannot be recycled. Pop in the compost bin instead. Only clean paper can be recycled.

Cleaning schedule

DOES ANYONE LIKE CLEANING? I CERTAINLY DON'T. I FIND IT TEDIOUS AND I'D MUCH RATHER SPEND MY TIME DOING SOMETHING MORE ENJOYABLE.

I used to leave cleaning my home until the weekend, cramming it all in between doing the laundry, ironing and grocery shopping. It meant that every weekend, the time I should have been relaxing was instead spent feeling stressed and completely overwhelmed by all the chores that needed to be done. Leaving the chores to mount up over a week also meant that I'd often have to resort to using industrial-strength cleaning supplies to get through the dirt that had accumulated. Now I only clean using natural products (see page 52) and it generally takes me only 10–15 minutes on a daily basis to keep on top of things. By implementing a weekly schedule,

my home is far easier to maintain. Cleaning has simply become part of my daily routine and I've found that I use far fewer products and save money, too. And by keeping on top of things I no longer need to resort to using more toxic cleaning products in my home.

When devising your own eco cleaning schedule, it's important to work out a few details first – spend some time assessing your own home, work out what needs to be cleaned and how much time you have available. If you have a large family home with several bedrooms or bathrooms, then it's going to take more work and time than a one-bedroom apartment. It may be easier to do all your cleaning and chores on a weekend if time is precious on workdays, or if you are based at home it may be possible to fit daily tasks in as part of your routine. If you have children, get them involved too by encouraging them to do some of the chores in their bedrooms, like stripping the beds, tidying up or dusting. Don't worry about including rooms that aren't used regularly, such as a guest bedroom or a study, and simply focus on the areas you frequently use.

Some chores need to be done daily – wiping down countertops, washing the dishes and cleaning up any spillages. I also find it's a good idea to wipe around the bathroom sink each morning with a cotton cloth as soap scum can be harder to shift if allowed to accumulate. For weekly jobs I follow the cleaning schedule which I've listed opposite.

Of course, life sometimes gets in the way and I postpone a task until another day or even move it to the next week, but I know I'll get back on track and things won't slide for long. I live in a small house with two bedrooms and one bathroom and this schedule works for our home, but your schedule will probably look very different.

WEEKLY SCHEDULE

Monday – kitchen: clean the oven and hob. Scrub sink and draining board. Wipe down appliances.

Tuesday – living room: dust all surfaces. Vacuum house.

Wednesday – bathroom: clean sink, toilet, bath and shower.

Thursday – main bedroom: strip beds, clean mirrors and dust.

Friday – second bedroom: strip beds and dust.

Green household essentials

So many of us use ecological detergents and cleaning products as a matter of course, without also thinking about the household tools we use to apply them. Sponges, cloths, brushes and scouring pads contain harmful synthetic dyes and are made from non-biodegradable plastics which end up in landfill sites. However, it's easy to make the switch to more sustainable tools, most of which are derived from plant-based ingredients like cotton, walnut shells, bamboo, loofah and coconut husk. All will get the job done effectively, are non-toxic and 100% biodegradable.

DISHWASHING BRUSHES

Instead of a plastic dish brush, choose a wooden-handled one with replacement heads containing bristles made from plant-based material. These are 100% biodegradable, unlike plastic brushes which can shed hairs that eventually end up in the ocean. Bamboo dishwashing brushes are also a good option as at the end of their lifespan they can be put in the compost bin (although if they have the nylon bristles, remove these first).

SCOURING PADS

Sometimes you need a scouring pad to deal with tough stains or burnt-on food that cannot be removed by soaking in water. Most of the commercial ones readily available in the supermarket are made from plastic and chemically dyed.

Great alternatives are scouring pads made from plant-based materials – loofah and coconut are both sustainable, non-toxic and free from chemical dyes. Many of them can be composted too.

CLEANING CLOTHS

I like to use organic cotton cloths for cleaning worktops, sinks and tiles. I simply pop them in the washing machine after I've used them and once they have got too shabby, I can put them into my compost bin as cotton is biodegradable.

TOILET BRUSH

I use a wooden toilet brush made with natural bristles. As with dishwashing brushes (see opposite), if any of the bristles come away they are biodegradable and won't cause harm to aquatic lifeforms, unlike plastic toilet brushes.

PAPER TOWELS

Ordinary paper towels can be wasteful as they generally get used once and then thrown in the bin. However, if you only use the sheets to mop up food spillages, then these can be popped in the compost bin. A good eco alternative is to buy bamboo paper towels which are reusable and biodegradable. Bamboo is extremely strong and will soak up more than ten times the liquid that regular towels can. You simply mop up any spillages or use it for cleaning and then pop it in the washing machine. When it's come to the end of its lifespan, you can add it to the compost bin too. Each sheet can be reused up to eighty times and can then be added to the compost bin.

Switch to natural cleaning

Have a look at the cleaning products in your kitchen cupboard or on any supermarket shelf and read the labels on products you use regularly. You'll probably see a big exclamation mark highlighting the possible risks from some ingredients to your health or the environment. These warning signs turn up on almost everything – washing powders, air fresheners, bathroom cleaners, multi-surface sprays and even washing-up liquids. Most of the ingredients are derived from non-renewable resources like petroleum and are not biodegradable. Many of these products also contain carcinogens, reproductive toxins, mood-altering chemicals and hormone disrupters, all of which have serious long-term health implications. Recent studies have shown that air pollution from cleaning and personal products now poses a greater risk to our health and the environment than car emissions do.

When you switch to green cleaning, you'll be safe in the knowledge that what you are using won't harm you, your family, your pets or the environment. Reducing the amount of toxins in the home often leads to improved wellbeing and many people find that allergies, headaches and skin conditions can be alleviated too. My son used to sneeze a lot in the house and would take an antihistamine tablet to control it, but since I've stopped using conventional cleaning products, he hasn't needed them.

Every product I now use to clean my home is free from harmful chemicals, environmentally friendly and good for my family's health and wellbeing. They save me money as they are cheaper to buy than conventional products and as they perform a multitude of tasks, I don't need to buy so many products. They also dramatically reduce the amount of plastic used as many come in glass bottles or cardboard packaging.

Making the change to green cleaning can seem overwhelming at first as the internet is full of conflicting information about what supplies to use and where, as well as using different terminology for what turns out to be the same product. I use only three things regularly and they do everything – bicarbonate of soda (baking soda), distilled white vinegar and castile soap. For some jobs, they work together and for others, I use them on their own.

Over the next couple of pages you'll find out why these three are particularly beneficial, and I have included a couple of recipe ideas for you to try. Occasionally I add a few drops of essential oils to the recipes but please be aware that some oils are toxic to pets. When you have become familiar with cleaning your home naturally, then you can add other ingredients to the mix, but for now I suggest starting simply with vinegar, castile soap and bicarbonate of soda (baking soda).

Natural cleaning products

Alongside castile soap (see page 54), I clean my home using vinegar and bicarbonate of soda (baking soda).

Vinegar is a great natural cleaner as it disinfects, cuts through grease and deodorizes. Distilled white vinegar is clear in colour and is often labelled as distilled malt vinegar (don't use the brown malt vinegar as that can stain). When used undiluted it's highly effective at killing bacteria and viruses. One word of warning: never use vinegar on granite or marble worktops as the acid can damage natural stone. It's also not a good idea to use it on wooden flooring. Bicarbonate of soda is also good for deodorizing and is equally brilliant to use as a scrubbing agent.

Both are nontoxic, biodegradable, extremely versatile and economical. Choose glass bottles of vinegar in the supermarket as these can easily

be recycled or buy in bulk – 5-litre (5-quart) canisters are available online. Large 1-kg (35-oz) packs of bicarbonate of soda are generally available from health food stores or online sources, and often come in cardboard boxes which can be easily recycled, too. Here are some of the ways I use these two products around my home:

WINDOW CLEANER

In a 1-litre (35-oz) spray bottle, add 300ml (1¼ cups) distilled white vinegar to the same quantity of water. Shake to mix well. Spray directly onto your windows and use a damp cloth or a squeegee to wipe them down. There's no need to rinse but use a dry cloth to wipe over the glass. This will leave your windows gleaming and streak-free. You can also add essential oils to the mix if you aren't keen on the vinegar aroma (although the smell does disappear quickly) – I usually add a few drops of lemon, lavender

and tea tree to the spray bottle.
However, don't add essential oils
if you have pets in the home.

WEED KILLER
Spray distilled white vinegar
directly on top of weeds. Reapply
on any new growth.

TOILET CLEANER
In a spray bottle, mix 250ml
(1 cup) distilled white vinegar
with a few drops of tea tree or
eucalyptus essential oil (if you have
pets, omit the essential oil) and
liberally spray the toilet seat, lid,
bowl, etc. Leave for 5 minutes.
Add a small handful of bicarbonate
of soda to the bowl and then scrub
with a toilet brush (see page 49).
Use a damp cloth to wipe the
vinegar spray from the seat.

DRAIN CLEANER
Drains often get blocked with
food and soap gunge. Pour a little
bicarbonate of soda down the
plughole and leave for 20 minutes.
Run hot water down the drain
to clear. I usually then spray the
sink area with my castile soap
multi-surface cleaner (see page 55)

and polish with a cloth. I do this
once a week as part of my regular
cleaning schedule.

OVEN CLEANER
Make sure the oven is off and cool.
Sprinkle a thin layer of bicarbonate
of soda over the bottom of the
oven. Lightly spray or sprinkle
some water over it and leave for an
hour. Use a scouring pad (see pages
48–49) to wipe away and lift off
any burnt-on food stains. I also use
this method on pans and dishes
that have burnt-on food

IN THE DUSTBIN (TRASH CAN)
For stinky bins, simply sprinkle
a little bicarbonate of soda (baking
soda) on the base and around the
insides. Leave for 20 minutes.
I usually lift the remnants off
with some paper towels (see page
49) and then wipe over the surface
with my castile soap multi-surface
cleaner (see page 55).

Castile soap

Castile soap is the third product I use for cleaning and it's my absolute favourite. Originating in Spain, the soap is made from all-natural vegetable oils (hemp, coconut, avocado or olive oil) and is free from nasty toxins like parabens, phthalates, sulphates and petroleum-based products. It's vegan as it contains no animal fats, nor is it tested on animals, as is the case with many commercial soap bars. It's completely biodegradable and as it has so many purposes, it reduces the need to buy other products, helping to reduce plastic consumption.

You can buy castile soap either in a concentrated liquid or in bar form. Both are good for different purposes and I tend to use the liquid for cleaning and the bar for body- and hand-washing. Castile soap is readily available from health food stores and online retailers, but check before you buy that nothing has been added to the ingredients list, such as colouring, preservatives or fragrances (other than essential oils). Some brands also use palm oil in the making of the soap, so look out for one that is sustainably sourced. As the liquid is extremely concentrated, you only need to use a little for each cleaning job so a bottle lasts a long time, making it great value for money.

Castile soap works best in softer water areas – using it as a cleaner with hard water can leave a white residue on shiny surfaces. This is due to the minerals in the water reacting with the soap and causing it to biodegrade. It's not harmful, but simply means you have to rinse the surface again. If you do live in a hard water area, you can combat this by using distilled or softened water instead of tap water.

Here's what I use it for around
my home:

DISHWASHING LIQUID

Use in place of regular detergent in
a ratio of 1:10 concentrated liquid
castile soap to water. It won't
bubble like normal dishwashing
liquid, but I find it cleans even the
toughest of burnt-on food stains
on pans and dishes. Simply pour a
little of the concentrated soap onto
the stain and leave for 10 minutes,
then scrub with a scouring pad
(see page 48–49).

MOPPING THE FLOOR

Add 50ml (3 tablespoons)
concentrated liquid castile soap
to a bucket of warm water. Clean
the floor using either a cotton
mop, floor cloth or a scrubbing
brush. No need to rinse. Don't use
on floors that have been recently
waxed as the soap can remove it.

MULTI-SURFACE CLEANER

Fill a clean 1-litre (35-oz) spray
bottle with tap water (or distilled/
softened water if you live in a
hard water area). Add 50ml
(3 tablespoons) concentrated liquid
castile soap. You can also add a few
drops of essential oils to the mix
if you prefer a scented product —
tea tree is a good choice for this
spray as it has natural antibacterial
properties, but be aware that some
essential oils are toxic to pets.
Spray lightly, then wipe off. I use
it on my kitchen worktops, sink
and the dining table.

SHOWER CURTAIN CLEANER

Over time my cotton shower
curtain gets grubby with mildew.
I used to pop it in the washing
machine with some stain remover,
but it was never particularly
effective. Now I use a little
concentrated soap on the stain,
rub the fabric together and then
wash in the machine. It comes
out much cleaner and there is
no mildew either.

Eco laundry

Look after your washing machine – there's nothing more frustrating than doing a load of laundry only for it to come out with dirty marks and sticky residue from powder build-ups. Running a cleaning programme on your machine and clearing out the filter once a month will to help prevent mould and bad odours developing. I also scrub out the dispenser drawer after running the programme, using an old toothbrush and liquid castile soap to remove all the gunky bits. Regular maintenance reduces the need to buy and use chemical-laden products to clean out the machine.

FILL UP THE MACHINE

Wait until you have a full load of laundry before you do a wash. It's more energy efficient and you'll use less product. If you need to wash a smaller load of laundry, choose a shorter cycle or use the half-load option, if your machine has it.

TEMPERATURE

Washing at 30°C (90°F) is commonly known to be a good temperature for energy efficiency. Some machines now have a 20°C (70°F) option which will save money and energy, as well as cleaning your clothes.

STAIN REMOVER

It's best to deal with the stain as soon as it occurs, and a bar of castile soap (see page 54) works well for this. Saturate the stain with cold water and scrub with the soap. Rinse and repeat if necessary, then machine wash as normal.

For perspiration marks under the arms of cotton shirts or tops, fill a basin with hot water and 200g (1 cup) bicarbonate of soda (baking soda). Soak for at least an hour or overnight, then machine wash as normal.

POWDER OR LIQUIDS

Opt for an eco-friendly brand that's not tested on animals, uses plant-derived ingredients, and is free from harmful phosphates, optical brighteners and chlorine bleach. Always use the correct amount of powder/liquid according to the label as using more doesn't make your laundry any cleaner and you are simply wasting product. Many eco brands now come in a concentrated form and have a special dosing cap that measures out the correct amount of liquid for each load. You can often buy eco washing powder or liquid in bulk, which means there is less plastic packaging to worry about, too. Some healthfood and zero-waste stores (see pages 68–69) now offer refill stations for some of the most popular eco brands, where you can fill up your own container.

FABRIC CONDITIONER

Like washing powder, opt for an eco-friendly brand that isn't tested on animals and uses plant-derived ingredients. If you can find a brand that uses essential oils rather than synthetic fragrances to scent your laundry, that's even better.

continued »

SOAP NUTS

If you are looking for a natural zero-waste option, these are a great choice. Known as soap berries, they are derived from the lychee family and have been around for thousands of years. They are dried fruit shells containing a natural soap called saponin, which is released when they meet water. You simply pop a small handful of the nuts in a wash bag and add them to the drum of the washing machine. They can be used several times before replacing, and you can put the used ones in the compost. Soap nuts are unscented and hypo-allergenic, but they are not particularly efficient at dealing with tough stains.

WASHING EGG/BALL

Another good zero-waste option is using a set of eco-friendly washing eggs/balls. These are unscented and filled with pellets made from minerals and plant-derived ingredients. They are vegan, hypo-allergenic and great for sensitive skin. Eco eggs/balls can be used for hundreds of washes, making them very cost effective too.

MICROFIBRES

When washing clothing made with microfibres (fleeces, acrylic sweaters, synthetic jackets, etc), tiny fibres are released from them into the waste water. These eventually end up in rivers, lakes and oceans where they can harm the aquatic life. Investing in a microfibre-catching laundry ball or a special mesh bag can capture these tiny fibres and prevent them escaping into the water supply.

DRY CLEANING

Most dry cleaning involves using a harmful solvent known as perchloroethylene to clean clothing. However, there are an increasing number of companies offering 'green cleaning' solutions which use non-toxic, environmentally friendly options. Look online for eco dry cleaning companies near you.

AIR DRYING

Hang your washing outside in the sunshine or on a clothes rack indoors to dry. You'll save money, energy and it's gentler for fabrics, zips and delicate items.

How to make your own natural washing powder

Making your own washing powder takes very little time and you only need two ingredients – castile soap (see page 54) and soda crystals (washing soda). Traditionally used to launder before modern detergents were invented, soda crystals cut through grease, deal with tough stains and prevent limescale from accumulating in your machine. This recipe makes enough for approximately 8 washes.

MAKES 1 JAR
YOU WILL NEED:

» 500g (2½ cups) soda crystals/washing soda
» 1 bar natural castile soap
» Food processor with grater attachment or a hand grater
» 1 jar or container with lid for storage

1 Pour the soda crystals/washing soda into a large bowl.

2 Grate the soap bar in the food processor or by hand. I like to grate my bar on the finest setting/hole size as it provides a better ratio of soap flakes to crystals.

3 Add to the soda crystals/washing soda and mix well.

4 Pour into your container to store.

TO USE: (IN FRONT LOADING MACHINES)

1 I use 2 tablespoons of washing powder for each full load of laundry.

2 Add the powder to the dispenser drawer or directly in the drum of the washing machine.

Eat Green

'If more of us valued food and cheer and song above hoarded gold, it would be a merrier world.'

J.R.R. Tolkien

Eat green

As well as food, this chapter also covers our kitchens and shopping habits. They are all connected, each playing an important role in adopting a greener lifestyle.

The most effective way to be greener in the kitchen is to address the amount of food we throw away. Most wasted food heads to landfill where it gradually rots, releasing methane – a gas more damaging to the environment than carbon dioxide. In the US, 150,000 tons of food are thrown away by households daily (source: via the *Guardian*/based on a study from the US Department of Agriculture). In France, the government has recently passed a bill forcing supermarkets to donate to charity food that is approaching its best before date, aiming to significantly reduce the 7 million tons of food waste it produces each year. Germany produces over 10 million tons of food waste, the Netherlands over 9 million and the UK throws away over 14 million tons of food every year (source: Eurostat).

The average family with children in the UK gets rid of £700 of unused food every year (source: WRAP) – that's quite a sum of money that could easily be spent on something better. I find one of the best ways to think about food waste is to put a value on it – how much has it cost you to pour that milk down the sink or throw all those apples in the bin? Picture it as actual cash and you might be less likely to get rid of it and more inclined to use it up instead.

Over the next few pages you'll find some tips to help reduce waste, get creative with your leftovers and make more considered choices when you go grocery shopping.

Meal planning

Taking the time to plan your meals and write a shopping list not only helps to prevent future food waste, but can save you lots of money too. Once a week, my husband and I sit down together and run through the meals we plan to cook. It's not an easy task as he works shifts and often eats at a different time from us, so we try to come up with meals that can be reheated or cooked quickly. We all live busy lives and the main thing is to be realistic – if you haven't the time or the energy to cook every day, then incorporate that into your meal plan.

AUDIT YOUR FRIDGE AND LARDER

Use up what's left first and make that your first meal of the week. Put anything that needs eating at the front of the fridge or shelf, then it's less likely to be overlooked.

MEAL PLANNING

Make enough for two nights when you can. I like to cook a big pot of chilli, serve it on the first day with rice, then turn the leftovers into something different on the following night – enchiladas, nachos, tacos, etc.

STRUCTURE THE WEEK

If you can, designate a day for the same meal every week – for us, Monday is meat free, Tuesday is curry, Wednesday is stir fry, Thursday is chilli, Friday is pizza. Keep weekends free for cooking something different. Kids love this routine as they always know when they are getting their favourite meal.

CELEBRATE LEFTOVERS

Lots of things taste even better the next day and make great lunches. Alternatively, store leftovers in the freezer and you have an extra meal ready prepared for next week.

GET AHEAD WHEN YOU CAN

It's a good idea to prepare certain things in advance. I like to roast big trays of vegetables in a little olive oil, then cool and keep them in the fridge. Throughout the week, these can be added to pasta dishes and stews or used as pizza toppings. If you are making pasta sauces, meatballs, curries or soups, make enough for two meals and stick one in the freezer for later. This makes more economical use of heating the oven, too.

WRITE YOUR LIST

I put mine on the Notes app on my smartphone as I find it useful to delete each item on the list as I'm going around the supermarket. I can see straightaway if I've missed anything which stops me from having to make a return visit for forgotten items. This also prevents me making too many impulse buys.

WHEN YOU ARE SHOPPING

Grocery stores move the oldest products to the front of the shelves so if you are shopping for ingredients for meals you've planned to make a few days later, look for the products with the longest use-by-date at the rear of the display.

TRY TO AVOID TEMPTATION

It's easy to get carried away when you see lots of discounted items or multi-buy offers. However, if you can freeze it or store it in the cupboard for another meal, then pop it in your basket.

WE ALL LIVE BUSY LIVES AND THE MAIN THING IS TO BE REALISTIC — IF YOU HAVEN'T THE TIME OR THE ENERGY TO COOK EVERY DAY, THEN INCORPORATE THAT INTO YOUR MEAL PLAN.

Shop local for fresh ingredients

When my son was a toddler I was keen to give him the best food I could possibly find. I invested in an organic box scheme, with fresh fruit and vegetables regularly delivered to my home. Whilst the produce all tasted great, I was disappointed that the majority had travelled vast distances to reach my plate. I went looking for a local alternative and after a quick internet search, I found a market garden only five minutes from my house. It was a place I'd driven past for years, yet never really acknowledged. I called in, had a lovely chat with the owner and tasted some of their home-grown lettuce. At that time I had no idea that that visit would alter the way I shop and change my life forever, as several years later I ended up working there. Seeing how much physical and emotional effort goes into running a farm or a market garden makes you appreciate food so much more.

Look for local growers selling direct from farm shops or at farmers' markets. Search online for 'farmers' markets near me'. I also like to include a visit to a farmers' market when I go on holiday as there is nothing better than sampling the fresh produce grown in the region you are staying in. 'Pick your own' is also a great way to support local growers and stock up on summer produce, too.

Why shop local?

IT'S BETTER FOR THE ENVIRONMENT

Buying fresh food from a local grower or farmer helps to reduce your carbon footprint substantially as there is no need for any transportation, food miles or refrigeration. Talk to the farmer or grower about their methods or use of pesticides – most will be happy to answer your questions. Many farmers or growers also offer a home delivery service, cutting down the need for more vehicles on the road too.

IT HELPS THE LOCAL ECONOMY

Businesses stay open, grow, employ local people and pass on traditional skills. Local businesses use the services of other local trades for printing, accounts, design and maintenance, which helps to strengthen the entire community.

FOOD IS FRESHER

With very little processing, packaging or transportation to consider, most fruit and vegetables will be picked fresh and immediately sold to customers. The difference in taste is incredible and the nutrient levels are significantly higher too.

IT BENEFITS THE LOCAL WILDLIFE

Fields, ponds, meadows and woodland encourage biodiversity and provide shelter for many species. Nature loses these precious commodities if farms are lost to property development.

Buy in bulk

WE ARE ALL LOOKING FOR
WAYS TO REDUCE OUR
RELIANCE ON PLASTICS,
AND ONE EASY WAY TO
DO THIS IS TO BUY SOME
GROCERIES IN BULK.

ASIAN SUPERMARKETS OR INDIAN GROCERY STORES

These are brilliant for huge sacks or bags of rice, grains, spices, noodles and dried pulses. Great value for money and as they are products that don't spoil easily, they will keep for a long time.

COFFEE

Most coffee roasters will sell their beans in 1-kg (2lb 4-oz) bags and will also grind the coffee to your specifications (see page 86). Look for local roasting companies where you can collect the beans rather than having them delivered, too.

FLOUR

If you make a lot of bread or love to bake, buying flour in bulk is a great way to save money and use less packaging. Supermarkets tend to sell 1kg (2lb 4oz) as the largest size, but flour mills sell their flours direct to consumers in 2.5-kg (5½-lb) bags, 16-kg (35-lb) bags and 25-kg (55-lb) sacks.

TEA

If you permanently have a cup of tea on the go, then bulk buying loose tea leaves is a great option (see page 84). Many tea producers sell 400-g (14-oz) or 500-g (1lb 2-oz) packets, including white and green teas. We have a great local market stall that sells loose leaf tea in a range of sizes from 50g (¾oz) right up to 1-kg (2lb 4-oz) sacks and we can collect it from the stall. Search online for tea retailers near you or for delivery to your home.

ZERO-WASTE STORES

We are starting to see more zero-waste stores opening which allow consumers to take their own containers to fill (see page 74). Look online for a store near you but if there aren't any to be found, it's worth searching crowdfunding websites as many community-based projects are looking for support to start a zero-waste store in your town or city. Thankfully there are a few plastic-free stores starting to pop up on the internet, which offer groceries packaged in paper and available in bulk sizes. Search online for home delivery options.

FOOD-BUYING GROUPS

Buying in bulk is a great concept but if you haven't the storage space for huge sacks of flour or rice, consider setting up a food-buying group. The idea is that friends, families, neighbours or work colleagues set up a group to purchase wholesale groceries, then split the products and the cost between the members. Buying this way saves money and uses less transportation, and by using your own containers to take products home in, less packaging is used too.

Clean out your larder

I've often bought ingredients for a specific meal or to bake a cake, only using a little and leaving the remainder to live out its days in the larder. From exotic spices and nuts to chickpea flour, they have all ended up being thrown away when I've discovered they're months (or even years) out of date. I was also guilty of having cupboards so full that I'd not be able to find what I needed before going to the shops, which often resulted in buying duplicates and having three or four bags open all at the same time. Cleaning out the larder on a regular basis will help to stop this happening and remind you what you could be making use of for future meals. I aim to go through my larder once a month, taking everything out and wiping down the shelves with my liquid castile soap spray (see page 55). Then I take an inventory of what needs to be used up before I plan my shopping list for the coming week.

Try some of these ideas for using up leftover packets or cans in the larder:

NUTS

Walnuts, hazelnuts, cashew nuts and almonds all make a great base for pesto. Lightly toast them in a frying pan (skillet) and leave to cool. In a food processor, toss in the nuts, a handful of basil, a clove of garlic and some extra virgin olive

oil. Process to mix. You may need to add a little more oil to reach the consistency you prefer. Season and add some grated Parmesan cheese. Mix through hot pasta to serve.

CURRY PASTE

Make a pie from vegetables and add some curry paste to the sauce. Add to soups. Mix with natural yogurt and stir through new potatoes or roasted vegetables.

CANNED BEANS

Chickpeas (garbanzo beans), kidney beans and cannellini beans are all lovely popped in a salad. Add some mixed leaves, cherry tomatoes, feta cheese and some lemon oil dressing (see page 98). If you have some herbs to use up, pop them in too. I like to make up a big batch of this and use it to fill lunchtime flatbreads. Make your own baked beans by adding the beans to a tomato sauce of onions, garlic, smoked paprika, passata (crushed tomatoes) and thyme.

GRAINS

Couscous, quinoa and bulgar wheat are great for lunchboxes. Cook, then let cool before mixing in herbs, lemon oil and cooked frozen peas for a protein-packed lunch.

PORRIDGE OATS (ROLLED OATS)

Make overnight oat bircher muesli for breakfast. In a bowl, add 50g (½ cup) porridge oats, a few toasted seeds and nuts and then 100g (½ cup) low-fat natural Greek yogurt. Mix to combine, then pop in the fridge overnight. In the morning add a chopped banana or some mixed berries and top with a few more mixed seeds and nuts. Alternatively, add oats to toppings for sweet and savoury crumbles, or use to replace breadcrumbs for extra crunch when making meatballs or burgers.

Packaging

Plastic packaging is often hard to avoid, but there are ways to reduce our consumption. It's worth taking the time to look for alternatives to products you regularly buy in the supermarket and instead head to health food shops, markets and delicatessens as they often sell items loose or in less packaging. It's also good to consider what you could make instead of buying; for example, sandwiches and boxed salads are easy to prepare at home and save on packaging and money.

Alternatives to switch to

» *Cereals* Look for oats, granola and muesli that come in paper bags.

» *Coleslaw and dips* Rather than buying from the deli counter, make your own coleslaw, hummus and tzatziki. They only use a few ingredients and take less than 20 minutes to make. Perfect for using up leftovers too.

» *Condiments and deli* Avoid ketchups, mayonnaise and salad dressings that come in plastic squeezy bottles and choose the ones in glass jars instead. Head to the deli counter for olives, antipasti and cheeses, where you can ask to use your own container.

» *Fruit* Buying fruit loose is easiest and cheapest at the market. Most stall holders sell their produce by weight and positively encourage you to bring your own bags.

» *Honey* Avoid squeezy plastic bottles and opt for glass jars. Look for local producers too, where you can really taste the flowers the bees have been foraging on.

» *Milk and juice* Search online for local dairies that can deliver fresh milk and orange juice in glass bottles – these are thankfully on the increase as more customers are looking for alternatives to plastic.

» *Nut milks* Like juice cartons, these often come in packaging that can't be recycled at the kerbside (although this is dependent on where you live). Making your own is easy if you want to avoid all packaging. It's as simple as soaking the nuts in water overnight, then adding to a blender. You can sweeten the milk with dates and vanilla extract, if you wish. Blitz and then strain through a nut milk bag or a piece of muslin (cheesecloth). It will keep fresh in the fridge for a few days.

» *Pasta, noodles and rice* Look for pasta and rice in cardboard packaging. Choose noodles that come in cardboard or recyclable plastic pots.

» *Peanut butter* Choose butters in glass jars rather than plastic pots. Go large wherever possible, as it is more cost effective and you won't have to recycle as often.

» *Salad* Buy lettuce, tomatoes, cucumber, etc. separately, rather than a pre-prepared salad bowl. It's cheaper to buy salad this way as you'll be able to get several portions out of the loose ingredients. Add whatever extras you like – chicken, cheese, nuts or fish – and drizzle with a simple dressing. On page 98 you'll find my recipe for a simple lemon and thyme oil which makes every salad taste delicious.

» *Sugar substitutes* Opt for agave and maple syrup in glass jars instead of squeezy plastic bottles.

There are lots of great zero-waste bloggers compiling lists of shops around the world that support the movement, so wherever you live or may be travelling to, search online for bloggers in that area and you'll find a wealth of information.

IT'S WORTH TAKING THE TIME TO LOOK FOR ALTERNATIVES AS HEALTH FOOD STORES OR MARKETS OFTEN SELL ITEMS LOOSE OR IN LESS PACKAGING.

Take your own containers

Supermarkets and grocery stores are very aware that consumers are looking for products with less packaging, and many have started to allow customers to bring their own containers. Hopefully we will see all supermarket and grocery chains roll this policy out and make it an easy option for us all to cut down on our use of disposable plastics. If your local store won't allow this, ask to speak to the manager about your concerns, send an email to head office or question them via their social media channels. The more the issue is raised, the more likely that change will follow.

If your store does allow you to use your own and you are keen to get started, then here are some tips to get your plastic-free produce home safely.

GLASS CONTAINERS

Use glass containers and jars with lids, stainless steel containers or reuse plastic takeaway containers. Make sure they are clean, dry and can properly close. Weigh each one, including any lids and make a note. This is known as the tare weight, or the weight of the empty container. Write the tare weight on a sticky label or a piece of washi tape and attach to the lid. This information is needed by the staff to correctly weigh your produce and not charge you extra for the weight of your container.

DELI/BUTCHER/FISH COUNTER

Glass jars with screw-top lids or stainless steel containers work best as they are easier to clean after transporting wet items. As above, weigh your container at home first, including any lids and note the weight.

BREAD BAGS

If you like to buy fresh bread from a bakery or supermarket, ask them to put your loaf into a cotton or linen bread bag instead. If it's at the supermarket, they may issue a barcode sticker to identify the product for the cashier. Simply stick this on to your bread bag. Once you have got all your produce home, empty your containers and wash them. Store them in a basket or a box and pop them back in the car or a place where you will remember to pick them up on your next shop.

PRODUCE BAGS

Made from hemp or cotton, these small bags work well for loose fruit and vegetables. Choose mesh bags to make it easier for the cashier to see what's inside, so you don't hold up the queue as they peer inside each bag! Many come with a tare weight label attached that you can write on; if they don't or you choose to make your own bags, write the weight on the bag with a permanent marker.

Choose reusable shopping bags

Many of us have already switched from single-use plastic shopping bags to 'bags for life' – a tougher plastic bag that the supermarkets sell and will replace for another one if it rips or tears. It seems like a good idea in theory, but in practice many of them are still thrown away and end up in landfill. These plastic bags are made from non-renewables and they don't biodegrade. They use photo degradation to break down into tiny microplastics, which cause major harm to the environment, birds and wildlife.

It's an easy switch to choose a shopping bag that's made from a more sustainable material. The hardest thing about switching to a reusable bag is remembering to take them with you when you go shopping! Write a note reminding you to take your bags and stick it somewhere you will see before you leave the house. I find that setting a reminder on my phone works well for me as it sends an alert when I arrive at the supermarket to take my bags into the store.

ORGANIC COTTON SHOPPING BAGS

Choose an unbleached, natural coloured bag as no chemical dyes have been used on them. These bags are lightweight, durable, can hold a lot of groceries and they can be put in the washing machine if they get stained. I have several of these that I use for larger shops. They are biodegradable and compostable.

JUTE SHOPPING BAGS

Jute is a vegetable fibre that is spun into strong threads. It has a low carbon footprint and needs a lot less water to produce

than cotton so it's eco credentials are high. As a material for shopping bags, it's ideal as it is durable and extremely strong, so it can bear a lot of weight. However, it can only be sponged clean, and if you were unlucky enough to have something spill out in the bag, it would be far harder to get the fibres completely clean. It's biodegradable and compostable.

STRING BAGS

Made from organic cotton, string bags are very strong, durable and can stretch to accommodate a lot of groceries. I always keep a couple

of these in my bag as they take up very little room. However, I do find they get a little awkward to carry when they are full, so I tend to use mine for small shopping trips or bringing books back from the library.

PRODUCE BAGS

Invest in some small produce bags for loose fresh fruit and vegetables. Organic cotton mesh versions are ideal as they are breathable, allowing fruit and vegetables to stay fresh in the bag until you are ready to cook with them.

Dump the plastic wrap

Plastic wrap (cling film) is one of those useful everyday items that most of us have in our kitchens to cover leftovers and wrap sandwiches in. Unfortunately, it can't be recycled due to the combination of chemicals and resins in the plastic which can't be separated, and it ends up in landfill where it takes hundreds of years to degrade. Whilst it's easy to make simple changes to put leftovers in containers, it can be harder to find ways to protect sandwiches, especially those that need to go in kids' lunchboxes, but there are some good alternatives available.

WAX WRAPS

These work by bending the wax wrap around a sandwich or container, with the warmth from your hands naturally securing it in place. This creates a water-repellent seal which keeps your food fresh. They are reusable, but you need to wash them after every use with cold water only (don't use dishwashing liquid as this can strip the wax). Leave them to air dry. Perfect for kids' lunchboxes and to wrap sandwiches, but they are not suitable for hot foods. Wax wraps last for 6–12 months and are biodegradable and compostable. There are two options available: beeswax, which should come from sustainably managed hives, or plant wax, which is usually made from soy wax and is suitable for vegans. On page 80 you'll find instructions for making your own wax wraps.

BIODEGRADABLE PAPER SANDWICH BAGS

These are made from strong, unbleached paper, are greaseproof and can be reused several times.

Once they are finished, you can add them to your food waste or composting bin. A good option for younger children as they open easily.

RECYCLED FOIL

Recycled foil uses 95% less energy to produce than normal tin foil and it can be recycled again and again. Perfect for leftovers and wrapping sandwiches.

If you don't have any spare containers for leftovers:

BOWL COVERS

These are simply covers made from cotton that pop over the top of the bowl, with an elastic trim to hold it in place. They come in a range of sizes and are machine washable so can be used again and again.

USE A PLATE

Use what you have! A dinner plate or side plate will often fit over the top of a bowl and cover leftovers. Although if you have kids going in and out of the fridge, this can be precarious!

BUYING LOCAL

Buying locally at farmers markets and farm shops means you'll use less plastic packaging as most items are loose or unwrapped. Take your own containers to the butcher, fishmonger or deli.

KILNER/MASON JARS

Ideal for storing fruit and vegetables that have been partly used/cut. Pop a little water in the bottom of the jar and store chopped carrots, courgettes, peppers, kale and broccoli. Keep checking the water to make sure it isn't going too brown and refresh when necessary. Glass jars with lids are particularly useful for keeping chopped or cut onions fresh.

REUSE

Takeaway containers made of foil can be washed and reused to store leftovers. Jam and mayonnaise jars can be washed and reused to store pulses, coffee beans, spices and loose-leaf teas. Ice cream containers can be washed and are ideal to store cakes, biscuits and rolls. Use a clean butter or margarine tub to store homemade dips or sauces.

continued »

How to make your own beeswax wraps

Making your own wraps is a very simple process. You can use old pillowcases or sheets if they are 100% cotton, or alternatively buy a couple of meters (yards) of fabric or a mixed pack of fat quarters (smaller pieces of fabric, often sold for patchwork and quilting). It's important to buy a new paintbrush and grater exclusively for this purpose (you won't want to grate cheese with it afterwards!).

It's worth noting that unlike shop-bought beeswax or plant wraps, these won't stick or 'cling'.

You simply wrap and fold under instead. The addition of tree resin and jojoba oil in the mass-market wraps is what gives them more of a plastic-wrap feel.

I find that one stick of beeswax makes three small wraps suitable for sandwiches. You will need a lot more beeswax if you want to make large sizes for bread or baked goods.

YOU WILL NEED

» 100% cotton fabric
» Greaseproof paper
» Baking sheet
» 1 stick of beeswax
» Grater
» Paintbrush

1 Preheat the oven to 140°C/275°F/Gas 1. Line a baking sheet with greaseproof paper.

2 Press your fabric flat. Cut your fabric into various sizes – small pieces for sandwiches or fruit, slightly larger pieces for leftovers. Place the fabric on top of the greaseproof paper. If you are using a printed fabric, place the print side face down on the greaseproof paper. You want to coat the non-printed side with the wax. Grate the beeswax on to the top of the fabric. Place in the preheated oven for 3–4 minutes until the wax just melts.

3 Remove from the oven and using the paintbrush, spread the melted wax over the fabric. If there are any gaps, grate over a little more wax and pop back in the oven.

4 Repeat the process until you have a wrap that is fully covered in wax. Hang on the washing line to dry.

The wraps can be used as soon as the wax has dried. To reuse, rinse them in cold water and if they need a more thorough clean, use a little liquid castile soap (see page 54) and hang on the line to dry. They will last 3–4 months.

Switch to an eco water bottle

Making plastic bottles for water or soft drinks requires vast quantities of oil, generates millions of tonnes of carbon dioxide and uses lots of energy. It also takes water to make bottled water as it's used in the production process! Then comes the waste factor – single use plastic bottles can end up in the sea, causing serious harm to marine life, or dumped in landfill where they take hundreds of years to degrade. Switching to an eco-water bottle is easy and there are several options available.

BPA AND PHTHALATE-FREE REUSABLE PLASTIC

These are relatively inexpensive, lightweight and widely available in supermarkets. However, they can deteriorate quickly, are difficult to clean, often develop bad odours and can harbour bacteria. Their lack of durability means they are often sent to landfill as they aren't recyclable. Most bottles are dishwasher safe.

ALUMINIUM BOTTLES

Relatively inexpensive, lightweight and durable, these have a plastic liner as aluminium can react with liquids. They can't go in the dishwasher and as they are made with mixed materials they are not recyclable.

STAINLESS STEEL

These are non-reactive with liquids, lightweight, and very durable but more expensive. Most stainless-steel bottles for adults and kids are dishwasher safe, but double check before you buy. Generally not recyclable.

GLASS BOTTLES

100% recyclable and sustainable, these won't impart any other flavours into your water and are dishwasher safe. Look for bottles made from borosilicate glass which are light, durable and temperature resistant rather than soda lime glass ones which don't handle extreme changes in heat and are also susceptible to shock.

KIDS' BOTTLES

Look for bottles that can adapt as your child grows. Many companies make a range of accessories such as sippy cups, detachable straws or sports caps which mean the bottle can be used for years to come.

HANDWASHING BOTTLES

Wash in warm, soapy water after every use and look for a set of bottle brushes in a variety of sizes so that you can get into those hard-to-reach areas that can harbour bacteria.

FLAVOURED WATERS

I try to drink as much water as I can during the day and often add some fresh fruit or herbs to make it more interesting. You can find bottles that have an insert for infusing the water, but I find it just as easy to use a big jug that

I can keep in the fridge. Make sure you wash your fruits and herbs before you use them.

To get the best out of any flavoured water it's best to pop the fruit and/or herbs into your jug and then press down on them with a spoon. This helps to release the juice and the flavour. Pour your water over the fruit mix and give it all a stir. Leave overnight in the fridge for optimum flavour and strain before serving.

Try some of these combinations:

» *Raspberry, lime & mint:* ten raspberries, two fresh mint leaves, one sliced lime.

» *Pineapple & thyme:* half a small pineapple chopped into chunks and two sprigs of fresh thyme.

» *Strawberry, orange & basil:* ten strawberries, one sliced orange and two fresh basil leaves.

» *Blueberry & peach:* ten blueberries, two chopped peaches.

Tea

We love the convenience of using teabags as it makes the process of tea-making effortless. However, many teabags are made with small amounts of plastic so as they biodegrade, they leave tiny microplastics behind. Thankfully, many of the bigger tea producers have realized that customers don't want plastics in their cuppa and are looking at sourcing alternative manufacturing materials. Until they are fully plastic free and completely biodegradable, it's worth making the simple change to loose-leaf tea.

BUY LOOSE-LEAF TEA

Choose loose-leaf teas in cardboard boxes or tins. Look for local tea merchants or health food stores where you can buy in bulk (see page 68). It saves money, too, as you can get several cups out of a single teapot or infuser opposite.

TEAPOTS

Look for teapots with a built-in infuser. You fill the holder with loose tea, pour hot water in and the tea is made.

MUG INFUSERS

Ideal for using loose-leaf tea in the office, this comes with a removable infuser and a lid. The tea leaves go in the infuser, you pour in the water and brew. When it's ready, remove the infuser and sit it on the lid to contain any drips.

INFUSERS

Also handy for individual cups or mugs of tea, these are made of a fine mesh and shaped like a globe. Give it a quick rinse with cold water before you fill it with loose-leaf tea as this helps prevent tea leaves escaping through any tiny gaps where it seals. Half-fill the infuser with tea, immerse in a cup of hot water and brew to your desired strength.

FILL YOUR OWN TEABAGS

If you like the convenience of a teabag or you want to brew teas with herbs from your garden, try making your own teabags. Source reusable bags produced from unbleached, food-grade cotton muslin. Simply pop your tea leaves into the little pouch, pull the drawstring to close the pouch and brew as normal. Once you are done, scrape the leaves out into the compost bin, turn the bag inside out and rinse under cold water.

Alternatively, choose single-use bags made from unbleached paper or plant fibres and pop in the food waste bin or compost them when you are done.

HERBAL TEA

Making tea with fresh mint from the garden is one of life's simple pleasures. You can use any variety of mint and there are lots to choose from – garden, apple, chocolate, strawberry, lemon, orange, peppermint, Moroccan and my own personal favourite, ginger mint. If you don't have any growing in the garden, choose a packet or a pot of fresh mint from the grocery store or market. Mint tea is lovely served hot but equally nice left to cool then poured over ice with a slice of lemon and orange.

For one cup of tea, all you need is six to eight fresh and washed ginger mint leaves plus some honey or sugar to sweeten. Pop your leaves into a clean mug. Boil the kettle, filling it with only what water you need and pour the boiling water over the ginger mint leaves. Infuse for five minutes then remove the leaves, adding a little honey or sugar to taste.

Coffee

With the ever-increasing popularity of coffee culture, retail chains, independents and home-brewing systmes have seen sales soar and the pressure on production has intensified. This rise in demand has led to a significant increase in the use of more harmful production methods, land degradation and deforestation.

The cheaper the bean, the more likely it has been grown by monocropping or full sun crop methods, causing soil erosion, intensive use of insecticides and lack of biodiversity. If you are a regular drinker of coffee like I am, then it pays to make considered choices when we are buying it.

GREEN UP YOUR COFFEE

Choose coffee beans that have been produced fairly and sustainably. Look for brands certified by the Rainforest Alliance and the Fairtrade Foundation as these organizations offer coffee farmers support with social, economic and environmental practices.

GRIND YOUR OWN BEANS

If you choose coffee beans over ground, then not only will you save money as they are less expensive, but you'll save on energy too. Grind your own beans by hand simply by turning the handle of a grinder – the smell is incredible, and it's a good work out!

BREWING

Electric kettles are by far the most energy efficient when it comes to brewing. The greenest way to make coffee is to only boil what water you need and then use it for instant coffee, a French press or a single drip method with a reusable filter rather than single use paper filters (although these can be composted). Alternatively, opt for the cold-brew method using cold water only.

COFFEE PODS

Every single day, millions of single-use coffee pods are thrown away and end up in landfill. These pods will take hundreds of years to break down, releasing methane into the atmosphere as they do so. Most of them are not recyclable as they are made from mixed materials that can't be easily separated. Choose brands that offer plant-based compostable pods or reusable stainless-steel capsules which you fill with your own ground coffee.

TAKE YOUR OWN COFFEE CUP/TRAVEL MUG

Around 2.5 billion coffee cups end up in landfill every year. Thankfully many major coffee chains are starting to address this issue by looking at ways to make their disposable cups more environmentally friendly and offering a discount to customers who bring their own. If you regularly pick up a coffee to go, then switch from a single-use cup to a reusable one or a travel mug. There are lots of great options available – bamboo, glass and stainless steel are all good choices.

Most come in a selection of sizes too, depending on which coffee you drink – perfect if you are an espresso or flat white fan and you only need a little cup.

Here are some tips for recycling your coffee grounds:

» *Compost* Add them to your compost bin, wormery or bokashi bin.

» *Garden fertilizer* Sprinkle used grounds directly onto the soil, then mix in well.

» *Hair* Rub a handful of used coffee grounds into your hair, leave for a few minutes, then shampoo and rinse as normal. This treatment enhances and darkens natural hair colours, so avoid if you have lighter coloured hair.

» *Body scrub* Mix with brown sugar and coconut oil to make an exfoliating scrub to treat cellulite. Look online for recipes.

» *Natural dye* Make wrapping paper and greetings cards from paper dyed with used coffee grounds. Look for tutorials online.

Eat seasonally

As a child growing up in the 1970s, we only ever ate peaches in the summer, and it was a treat to bite into the ripe fruit and revel in its flavour. We would never have eaten them in the winter unless they came out of a can! Now you can buy them all year around, but if you eat one in winter, there's a good chance it will be as hard as a cricket ball and missing that depth of flavour. Produce grown out of season is picked before it's ready, refrigerated and then shipped or flown thousands of miles. When it finally arrives at its destination, it's often heated in hot houses to ripen artificially before it hits the supermarket shelves.

Fruit and vegetables taste so much better when they have just been picked. Spring brings us fresh peas, asparagus and new potatoes, while summer fruits like strawberries and raspberries that have

ripened in the sunshine just can't be beaten. In autumn we welcome striped squashes and vibrant pumpkins, before winter showers us with Brussels sprouts and hearty root vegetables.

Choosing to shop and eat this way helps the environment as less transportation, less refrigeration and less hot-house use is required. It can also be cheaper to buy food that's in season as it's abundant.

Freezing fresh produce

I also like to buy a little more produce when it's in season so that I can freeze some to eat later in the year, rather than relying on imported produce. Here's how to prepare fruits and vegetables for freezing:

» *Asparagus* Snap the ends off thicker stems and blanch in boiling water for 2–4 minutes. Plunge into cold water, drain and freeze. Use within 8–12 months.

» *Broccoli, brussels sprouts, cauliflower, green beans, kale* Blanch in boiling water for 2–4 minutes. Plunge into a bowl of cold water, drain and then freeze. Use within 12 months.

To freeze fruits, line a baking sheet with some greaseproof paper. Spread the prepared fruit (see below) onto the paper, making sure they don't overlap. Pop in the freezer for a couple of hours. When frozen hard, transfer to a freezer bag or container and write the date on a label. Fruits will keep well for 3 months.

» *Apples, pears* Peel, core and cut into slices. Freeze as above.

» *Figs* Wash and allow to dry. Freeze as above.

» *Plums* Wash, cut in half, stone. Freeze as above.

» *Rhubarb* Wash and slice into pieces. Freeze as above.

» *Strawberries* Wash, hull and chop into halves. Freeze as above.

Preserving produce

Jams, jellies, chutneys, and cordials are a great way to celebrate the seasons and they make wonderful gifts for Christmas. Making preserves isn't as difficult as it sounds, but it can take a little practice to get it right.

GOOD FRUITS FOR JAM MAKING
blackberries, damsons, figs, peaches, rhubarb*, strawberries

*Forced rhubarb also adds the best flavour to gin or vodka. Look online for recipes and buy a cheap, supermarket own brand gin or vodka to infuse.

GOOD VEGETABLES FOR PICKLING
Beetroot (beets), courgettes (zucchini), green beans, red cabbage.

How to make strawberry and elderflower jam

I had always assumed jam making would be a complicated process. The idea of sterilizing the jars and getting the right setting point seemed exhausting when it was a lot easier to buy a jar in the supermarket. I couldn't have been more wrong as once you get the hang of it, it's simple. In the depths of winter, there is nothing nicer than digging your spoon into a jar of this strawberry and elderflower jam – it instantly transports you back to sunny, summer days.

I like to use glass jars with clip-top lids and rubber seals for preserving as these can be used repeatedly. You can recycle old jam jars if you wish, but it's important to buy new lids and wax discs to ensure that no bacteria can enter the jar and spoil your jam. Don't add hot food to cold jars or cold food to hot jars as this can cause them to shatter.

» *Sterilizing* Preheat the oven to 130°C/250°F/Gas 1. Wash glass jars, lids and seals in warm, soapy water, then rinse. Put the jars and the lids (if they are glass ones) on a baking sheet and put in the oven for 30 minutes. Sterilize rubber seals and lids by soaking them in boiling water.

» *Temperature* The setting point for jam is 105°C/220°F. Using a sugar thermometer is the easiest way to check that your jam has reached the correct temperature. Alternatively, you can use the wrinkle test (follow the instructions in the method opposite).

» *Timing* As the jars need to sterilize for around 30 minutes (see above), I pop my jars in, then wait 20 minutes before I start heating my pan of fruit. After 10 minutes of boiling the jam, the jars will have had their 30 minutes and are ready to be filled.

MAKES 3 JARS

» 600g (6 cups) strawberries (hulled weight)
» 500g (2½ cups) jam sugar (this contains added pectin, which helps the jam to set)
» 50ml (3½ tablespoons) undiluted elderflower cordial

1 Put the washed and hulled strawberries into a large pan or jam pan. Cover with the jam sugar and stir to combine. Cover and leave overnight.

2 The next day, sterilize your jars, lids and rubber seals (see opposite for the method).

3 After 20 minutes, start heating the jam and bring to the boil. Keep boiling for 10 minutes. If using a sugar thermometer, turn off the heat at 105°C/220°F. If doing the wrinkle test, when you think the jam is ready, turn off the heat. Spoon a small amount on to a chilled saucer, allow it to cool (to avoid burning yourself) and then push your finger through the jam. If it wrinkles, it has reached the setting point. If not, turn the heat back on, simmer for 5 minutes and try again.

Leave to cool for a couple of minutes, then stir through the elderflower cordial.

4 Decant the jam into the hot sterilized jars and seal.

5 Keep in a cool, dark place. Once opened, keep in the fridge and use within 3 months.

Foraging

I love to head off on a foraging adventures, taking my basket and filling it with leaves, mushrooms and fruits. It's essential to learn how to identify which plants, berries and fungi you can pick safely as many are toxic. I've been on a foraging course with a local teacher and I really recommend doing something similar in your own area to ensure you are picking correctly.

It is vital to forage responsibly – don't forage on private land, don't take everything and leave some behind for wildlife and birds. If you are lucky enough to live by the coast, there are lots of seaweeds, samphire, clams and plants you can forage for too. Borrow or buy a book on wild food identification and don't eat anything unless you are 100% sure it's edible.

Remember to wash everything thoroughly, and don't forage too close to busy roads where car exhaust fumes can spoil the plants and fruits.

Here are some common edibles to get you started:

» *Blackberries* These are the fruits from the thorny, bramble bushes that grow rampant in woodland and hedgerows. They start off green, turn red, then deep purple and when finally ripe and ready to pick they are black. They are usually ripe from late summer through to early autumn. Use for crumbles, cakes, wine, vinegar and jams. Go prepared with a large container to fill as blackberries freeze well.

» *Dandelions* Use the flower heads in salads, the petals for wine and the young leaves in pesto. They grow abundantly in lawns, parks and gardens, but it's important not to pick any that may have been sprayed with pesticides. Ideally, it's best to pick them from your own garden.

» *Elderflowers* Flat topped, creamy white flowers which appear in early summer. The flowers and berries must be cooked before eating otherwise they are mildly toxic (cooking destroys the toxic chemicals). Use the flowers to make cordial, jellies, wine, tea, fritters and cakes. See pages 90–91 for my strawberry and elderflower jam recipe.

» *Nettles* Harvest in spring when they are young and before they flower. Wear gloves as they can really sting, but steaming and blanching destroys this. Make nettle pesto, tea, soup and risottos. Nettles have more vitamins and minerals than broccoli or spinach and are one of nature's superfoods.

» *Ramsons/Wild garlic* Found in woodland and hedgerows (often grows next to bluebells as they both prefer slightly acidic soils). You'll often smell this before you see it! Harvest the leaves, stems and flowers but not the bulbs. They wilt quickly after picking, so pop them in the fridge as soon as you can or use them straight away. Use to make garlic butter and in salads, breads, pesto, frittatas and tarts.

» *Sloes* These little purple berries are found on blackthorn bushes and are usually found in the hedgerows on country lanes,

continued »

although some bushes are grown in gardens as natural hedging. Blackthorns have sharp thorns and spectacular cream-coloured flowers in spring. Often confused with the hawthorn bush, it's simple to tell them apart – the blackthorn flowers before the leaves start to develop, unlike the hawthorn whose flowers follow the leaves. Native to the UK and Europe, blackthorn bushes have also been naturalized in North America, Australia and New Zealand. They have marble-sized fruits that appear in summer, starting off green before turning blue-black. Cut into one of the berries and you will see the flesh is green with a small plum-like stone in the centre. Pick after the first frosts in early autumn as this helps to soften the skin and release the juices. Make jams, vinegars and whisky.

» *Wild strawberries* Found in woodland and hedgerows, wild strawberries are tiny but bursting with flavour. Best served as they are or with cream. They are ready to pick in the summer months.

MAKING FLAVOURED GIN, VODKA OR WHISKY

Very simple, and needs few ingredients. The secret to a good bottle is patience as the longer you leave it, the more intoxicating the flavour. Decanted into miniatures, they make fantastic Christmas presents or wedding favours too. Sloe gin is my favourite, and there is nothing better than a little nip on a cold, winter night.

BEFORE YOU PICK

Borrow a wild food identification book from the library and take it with you when you head off to pick, or check out blogs or YouTube for videos from expert foragers.

How to make sloe gin

MAKES 2 LARGE JARS

» 70cl bottle gin
» 500g (1lb 2oz) sloes
» 250g (1¼ cups) caster (superfine) sugar
» 2 large Mason/Kilner jars with lids and rubber seals, sterilized (see page 90)
» Muslin cloth (cheesecloth)

1 Place the sloes in a large bowl and cover with water. Leave for 20 minutes to ensure that any leaves, dirt or insects have been removed from the berries.

2 Drain through a sieve and rinse. Pop them in a freezer bag and place in the freezer overnight (this splits the skin, releasing their natural juices).

3 The next day, fill one jar with the berries and cover with the sugar. Pour the bottle of gin over, seal tightly, then shake to mix. Store in a cool, dark place and shake once a week.

4 After three months, strain the liquid through a muslin cloth into a clean, sterilized bottle or jar. Enjoy!

If you keep hold of the sloes, they make a wonderful boozy addition to a crumble or you could dip them in chocolate!

TIP

If you can't find sloes, try these alternatives:

Bullace: a small wild plum, blue-black in colour and often mistaken for large sloes. They taste like greengages and they work well in gin and vodka.

Damsons: smaller than a plum, dark purple in colour and more oval in shape than a bullace or sloe. You can often find them in autumn at farmers' markets.

Grow your own

If you have room for a pot on
a balcony, a window box or a
hanging basket at your front
door, there are fruits, herbs and
vegetables that will grow happily
and provide you with home-grown
produce. And if you have no
outside space at all, there are still
lots of options to grow indoors in
containers on a windowsill.

**GROWING JUST ONE
THING IS A GREAT WAY
TO BE GREENER IN THE
KITCHEN.**

Every summer I like to grow
a couple of edibles in my tiny
city garden, using two foldaway
planters and two old fruit crates
for climbing beans, tomatoes,
strawberries and spinach. In the
colder months, I like to grow a
few things indoors too.

Indoor growing on the windowsill

Choose a pot or a window box at
least 10cm (4in) deep and make
sure to add some drainage holes to
the bottom (you'll need a saucer
too, to catch draining water). Fill
the container with a good multi-
purpose potting compost, leaving
3–4cm (1½in) clear at the top.
Water the compost and then sow
your seeds.

» *Baby salad leaves* Sow directly
into your container. Cover with a
thin layer of compost and water
regularly to keep the soil moist.
You may need to thin out the
leaves to stop overcrowding.
Harvest when the leaves are a few
inches tall and they will grow back
again. Keep lettuce out of the hot
sun as it can wilt.

» *Pea shoots* Pre-soak the peas in
water for 24 hours. Sow the peas
close together and cover with

compost, then water the surface. Keep watering every day in warm weather or every other day if it's cooler. After two weeks, the shoots should be ready to harvest. You may find you get a second crop too.

» *Rocket (arugula) and spinach*
Sow directly into your container. Cover with a thin layer of compost and water regularly to keep the soil moist. Baby leaves take around 3–4 weeks to grow.

Growing outdoors in pots

» *Edible flowers* Borage, calendula (marigolds), nasturtiums and violas will all grow happily in pots or a window box. Use borage, calendula and nasturtium flowers in salads. Violas are beautiful to decorate cakes or sprinkled over desserts and fruit salads. Nasturtium leaves also make a lovely peppery pesto.

» *French (green) beans* Choose dwarf varieties. Sow outdoors in late spring when the possibility of frost has passed. Plant them around the edges of a pot and in the centre plant a perennial or herb. Bees will love this too.

» *Herbs* Chamomile, mint, oregano, rosemary, sage and thyme all grow well in containers.

continued »

How to make lemon and thyme-infused oil

Whenever I need to perk up some home-grown or leftover salad leaves, this dressing is my go-to. It's also a great recipe for using up any lemons after you have juiced them as the peel flavours the oil.

MAKES 1 BOTTLE (250ML)

» 2 unwaxed lemons
» 250ml (1 cup) rapeseed (canola) oil
» 4–6 fresh sprigs of thyme or lemon thyme
» 1 bottle with a lid, sterilized (see page 90)

1 Wash the lemons and peel the skins. Put the peel and the oil into a small saucepan. Gently heat for 10 minutes, but do not to let it boil.

2 Take off the heat, add the thyme sprigs and allow to cool completely.

3 When cool, remove the thyme sprigs and the lemon peel. Transfer the flavoured oil to a sterilized glass jar or bottle. Keeps for 1 month.

Plant mint in a pot on its own as it grows very fast and prevents other herbs from thriving. Infused oils are a great way to use up excess or leftover herbs.

» *Strawberries* Buy several varieties as they fruit at different times and you can keep harvesting throughout the summer.

» *Tomatoes* Choose bush or tumbling varieties that grow well in containers or hanging baskets. Feed with an organic liquid seaweed fertilizer.

NATURAL FERTILIZER

Potassium, calcium and phosphorus are vital minerals needed for growing strong plants. Banana peels contain high quantities of these nutrients and they make a great fertilizer to encourage healthy crops. Use this homemade fertilizer on tomato, lettuce and vegetable plants. Roses also love this mix and will flourish if you add some chopped banana peel around their roots.

To make your own banana peel tea fertilizer you need a 1 litre (35-oz) glass jar and two organic banana skins (choose organic as they will not have been sprayed with harmful pesticides or herbicides).

Simply pop the two banana skins into the jar and then fill the jar with water (rainwater is best but water from the tap will work too). Cover the top of the jar with a cloth. Leave for 48 hours. Remove the peels and add them to the compost bin.

Alternatively, you can bury them directly into the soil for an extra nutritional boost. If you choose to bury the peels, make sure to dig down at least 10cm (4in) to prevent unwanted attention from vermin. Pop the liquid from the jar into a watering can and water your plants with your banana peel tea.

Tips to avoid food waste

The amount of food the average family throws away is staggering. Most of it ends up in landfill where it degrades very slowly, releasing harmful greenhouse gases into the atmosphere. It means that we are throwing our money away too, and as food prices continue to rise, it's only sensible that we do what we can to reduce our bills and waste.

Here are the most common foods that are thrown away every week and some ways to use them up:

BANANAS

Make a super-easy dessert by freezing ripe banana slices. Pop them into a food processor and keep pulsing until they resemble soft-serve ice cream, then add some chocolate chip pieces or a spoonful of peanut butter. Pour into a container and freeze until solid again. Also look online for recipes for banana bread, muffins and pancakes.

BREAD

No matter what kind of bread you buy, the loaf often becomes stale before you can finish it. If you buy uncut loaves, cut it into slices straight away and pop some of them in the freezer in a container or freezer bag. This also works with a regular sandwich loaf. Some people like to defrost the slices in the microwave for a couple of minutes, but I simply pop mine in the toaster. I also use the crusts to make breadcrumbs – simply stick them in the food processor and roughly chop, then use them when making burgers and meatballs or on pasta dishes.

MILK

Millions of glasses of milk are literally poured down the sink every week. Consider buying a smaller carton or look for a local dairy that offers home delivery in glass bottles. Alternatively, use up excess milk by making a batch of béchamel sauce and add some grated Cheddar cheese. Pop it in the freezer and you have a ready-made sauce for lasagne or cauliflower cheese ready for dinner.

POTATOES
Get ahead for roast dinners. Par-boil potatoes and arrange them on a baking sheet. Pop in the freezer until solid, then transfer to a freezer bag. They can be cooked from frozen. Use within a month. Leftover mashed potato can be frozen and will keep for a month (thaw before reheating). Potato peelings make great fries – simply toss them in a little olive oil, sprinkle with salt or cumin powder and bake in the oven for 10 minutes at 200°C/400°F/Gas 6 degrees until crispy.

SALAD BAGS
As consumers we love them for their convenience and variety of leaves. Unfortunately, the minute you open the bag, oxygen gets in and those pristine leaves start to turn to yellow slime. To make them last longer, place them in a colander and rinse with cold water. Drain and then wrap the leaves in a clean damp dish towel. Pop in the salad drawer of the fridge and they should remain fresh for a week.

CHEESE
Gather cheese offcuts and large crumbs and pop them in a freezer bag. Store in the freezer and add to the bag whenever you have some leftovers. These make a great sauce for macaroni or cauliflower cheese and work well on top of pizzas. Add the rind from Parmesan to soups and stews to give extra flavour. Turn leftover Cheddar into scones or make savoury cheese and chive dumplings to top casseroles and stews.

NATURAL/GREEK YOGHURT
Make your own coleslaw with chopped red onion, red cabbage, carrot ribbons and lemon juice. Add some mayo and natural yoghurt and season to taste. Or swirl some natural yoghurt through pasta instead of cream. Mix with jam or fruit coulis and pop in the freezer for a homemade frozen yoghurt dessert.

How to make your herbs last longer

Cooking and eating fresh herbs is one of life's great pleasures. There is nothing nicer than heading out to your own garden on a sunny day, cutting some fresh thyme and smelling its intoxicating aroma. In the middle of winter, this isn't an option so you have to buy them from the supermarket or greengrocer. You pop them in the fridge, use a little, then forget all about them so they promptly turn to mush in the salad drawer.

However, there are some ways to make them last longer:

LIVING HERBS

If you buy basil in the supermarket, opt for a pot as it will keep growing for a long time. Pop the plant on a sunny windowsill and keep it watered. When you want to use it, take the largest leaves off the top first, then look down the stem and you'll probably see two little leaf nodules sticking out. Make the cut just above those nodules. By doing this you help the plant to transfer energy up the stem and into those baby leaves, and in a week or so, you'll have fully grown basil leaves again. Keep repeating until the plant looks tired, then add to the compost heap.

PACKET HERBS

Thyme, rosemary, parsley and coriander (cilantro): take them out of the packet and strip off any low-growing leaves. Use them first or follow the instructions opposite for preserving. With the remaining stems, cut a little from the bottom and then pop into a glass of water, keeping only the stems and not the leaves submerged. Place in the fridge and they will usually keep fresh for a couple of weeks. Change the water in the glass every couple of days to keep them happy.

PRESERVING

This works for herbs in packets, pot grown or the garden. You need a couple of clean ice cube trays, some herbs and olive oil. Strip the leaves from the stalks and roughly chop. Half-fill each ice cube compartment with your chosen herb, then top with olive oil. Cover with beeswax wraps (see page 81) and pop in the freezer. Once they are frozen, you can transfer them to a separate container or freezer bag. These make the ideal base for cooking onions or garlic and there is no need to defrost them before heating in a pan. This method works best for oregano, rosemary, thyme and sage, but it's not as good for softer herbs like coriander (cilantro) or basil.

DRYING

Gather bunches of herbs from the garden or use a packet from the supermarket. Wash well and pat dry. Tie the stems together with some twine or an elastic band. Hang somewhere warm and dry, making sure the flowers and leaves point downwards.

Composting

One of the easiest ways to deal with food waste is to compost it. Many local authorities already help residents with this, offering special food scrap bins that they collect regularly and convert to compost.

Our local council sadly doesn't provide us with this, so instead we invested in a small compost bin for the back garden. It works well for us, providing vital nutrients to help improve the soil in the garden and means we don't have to send any food waste to landfill.

THINGS TO COMPOST

Fruit and vegetable scraps, eggshells, coffee grounds, loose-leaf tea, teabags (that are free from plastic, see page 84), paper towels, newspaper, hair from pets and humans, dried pet food and natural fibres like cotton or wool.

If you have only have a small outside space or no garden at all, there are still plenty of ways you can compost your food waste.

BOKASHI BINS

Ideal for indoor composting and available in small sizes too. You pop any food waste, cooked and uncooked, into the bin, sprinkle on a type of bran that contains good bacteria and then shut the lid. Repeat until the bin is completely full, then leave it to ferment for two weeks. Liquid feed is produced during the fermentation period and you can use this to water garden plants and houseplants as it's full of beneficial nutrients. During the two-week rest period, food waste is broken down into regular compost which can then be added to the garden, an existing compost bin or a wormery.

WORM COMPOSTING

Worms convert kitchen waste into nutrient-rich compost and a liquid fertilizer. A wormery is best kept in a sheltered area of the garden, a garage or a shed, as the worms don't like to get too hot or too cold. You can have a wormery indoors too and they are great for small spaces. Look online for a wealth of tutorials on how to make your own.

COLD COMPOSTING IN A BLENDER

Make instant compost in a blender. Throw fruit and vegetable scraps, eggshells, shredded newspaper and coffee grounds into the blender. Top with water and blend until puréed. Dig a small trench or hole in the garden and pour the liquid in. Cover it over with soil to prevent attracting rodents.

COMMUNITY COMPOST SCHEMES

If you would like to compost your food waste but haven't got the space or resources to do it yourself, there are compost schemes you can get involved with. These will often accept your food waste as part of their commitment to cut down on the amount of waste sent to landfill and produce compost that benefits the local community. Look online for local groups and freeze food scraps until you can donate them.

Slow Fashion

'*Buy less, choose well, make it last.*'
Vivienne Westwood

Slow fashion

Consumer demands for cheap clothing have placed an enormous strain on our planet, with fast fashion the second biggest polluter in the world, after the oil industry. Polyester is one of the most common fabrics and is essentially a plastic. The manufacturing of polyester uses millions of barrels of oil every year as it is a synthetic, petroleum-based fibre. It is carbon intensive and has double the carbon footprint of cotton, and it's not biodegradable. These synthetic fibres have also been found to shed tiny particles every time they are washed, releasing millions of microplastics into the water supply.

Billions of pieces of clothing are produced each year and are designed, created and sold to consumers as quickly as possible and at low prices. Traditionally there used to be two fashion collections a year; now, due to the fast fashion industry, there are 50 cycles of new collections released every year. Consumption of fast fashion is rising rapidly while the length of time an item is kept and the number of times it is worn are dramatically falling. Brands have also been left with huge quantities of unsold stock, contributing even more to landfill.

It's easy to get fooled into buying more cheap clothes. We buy because we believe it will make us happy or we'll look better. Shopping used to be my hobby and I filled many a basket with cheap t-shirts, tops and bags. I ran out of space for all my clothes, but now I don't shop like that at all. This doesn't happen overnight, and it takes a lot of willpower, but it does get easier. Over the next few pages you'll find some ways to help you organize your closet, work with what you already have and buy with intention.

Clean out your closet

We've all bought things that we liked on the clothes hanger, put them on a couple of times and decided that we don't really like them. Maybe they are not comfortable, they don't fit properly, or they simply don't work with the other clothes you own, so they get consigned to the back of the cupboard and promptly forgotten about. If you have a wardrobe or chest of drawers that is positively groaning with clothes, shoes and accessories, it's a good idea to clear it out and see what's really in there. Donating and getting rid of unwanted clothing is a great start to creating a greener wardrobe. You could also hold a clothes swapping party with your friends (see page 125).

How to clear out your closet

» Gather two boxes – one for donating and one for recyling.

» Remove everything from the closet but try to keep the piles together, so sweaters in one pile, dresses in another, etc.

» Once your closet is empty, give it a dust and a wipe down, ideally with some lavender oil to help deter moths. Give it a quick vacuum and leave it to air out.

» Go through each pile of clothing and decide if it's something you want to keep, donate or recycle (refer to the questions opposite to guide you). Put the item back in the wardrobe if you are keeping it or pop it in the relevant box if you are happy to part with it.

» Once you have finished going through all your items, take your donations to a local charity shop or put them in a clothing bin at the recycling centre.

» Recyle or throw out the contents of the other box or if they are cotton, turn them into handy rags to use for cleaning.

Questions to ask yourself

» How does it make you feel wearing it? If it's great, keep it. If not, get rid of it.

» Is it comfy, does it fit properly? If it's no, say goodbye.

» When was the last time you wore it? If it's more than a year, why do you keep hold of it?

» If it's damaged, is it worth getting it repaired? If it's a no, let it go.

» Is it useful or is there a good reason to keep it? This could be anything from maternity wear, sports equipment to return-to-work clothing. If it's a yes, keep it.

GETTING RID OF SENTIMENTAL ITEMS

Items like wedding dresses or clothing you may have an attachment to can be difficult to let go. My wedding dress was two sizes smaller than the clothes I currently wear and I knew I'd never wear it again, yet I was still reluctant to part with it. I eventually realized that by choosing to donate it, someone else could benefit from its beauty rather than it lurking in the back of my closet forever.

Dealing with moths

Although switching to clothing made from natural fibres is better for the environment, it can turn your wardrobe into an all-you-can-eat buffet for moths.

Moths thrive in dark, warm conditions and if spring is unseasonably hot, they will be prolific breeders. If your summer clothes have been in the closet throughout winter, you may find them full of holes when you bring them out in warm weather. Textile moths live for around 65 days, during which they lay over 50 eggs. Larvae burrow into the fibres of clothing, feasting on fabric.

If you see moths flying around your home or spot cocoons, it's likely you have an infestation. Rather than treat the problem with moth balls (essentially toxic chemicals), use natural remedies to get rid of them.

If you have moths in your closet:

» Clean out your closet (take everything out, vacuum and wipe down all surfaces with a damp cloth and a natural multi-surface cleaner (see page 55).

» Wash any natural fibre clothes.

» If you have a big enough freezer, wrap each item of clothing in a sealed bag and freeze for 48 hours. The freezing temperatures will kill the larvae.

» If you haven't got a big freezer, ironing clothing kills off the larvae and any moth eggs too.

» Moths are repelled by the natural oils in red cedarwood. Invest in cedarwood clothes hangers or cedarwood rings that fit over your current clothes hangers. Cedarwood rings, hangers and balls will work effectively for around three months. After that time, simply give them a light rub down with sandpaper and they will start to release their scent again.

» Put any off-season clothing in a sealed, breathable garment bag and add a ball of cedarwood.

» Don't put any dirty clothing back in the closet or drawers as moth larvae love to feast on sweat and food stains.

» Make dried herb sachets. Moths detest the aromas of strong herbs like lavender, rosemary and thyme. Gather bunches of these herbs from your garden, hang them in a dark place to dry out, then make up these sachets to put in your closet, cupboards and drawers. If you don't have a garden, you can easily find dried ones online.

How to make a natural moth repellent

YOU WILL NEED
» 1 large bunch of dried rosemary, lavender and thyme
» Reusable cotton spice bags or make your own from fabric scraps

1 Strip the flowers from the lavender stems, the needles from the rosemary sprigs and the leaves from the thyme sprigs and put them in a bowl. Mix well.

2 Scoop the mix into the cotton bags. Hang in closets, drawers and cupboards.

Mending and looking after your clothes

Buying less but better helps to reduce our impact on the environment. When we spend more money on an item of clothing, we'd ideally like it to last for a long time. Occasionally life gets in the way of that goal – we pull a thread in a beloved sweater sleeve, a hem comes down or our jeans get torn. It can be daunting if you don't know how to sew and it might seem expensive to take it to a professional, but some items can be relatively straightforward to repair at home.

HEMMING TAPE

This is brilliant for taking up trousers (pants) or repairing hems that have come loose. It works by bonding the fabric together without any need for stitching. Start by turning the garment inside out and fold over the length you want taking up. Cut a piece of tape to fit the hemline and insert it into the fold. Dampen a dish towel and place it over the area you have inserted the tape. Using a hot iron, press it down firmly on the dish towel. Repeat a couple of times, then remove the dish towel.

IRON-ON PATCHES FOR JEANS

Made from 100% cotton, these iron-on patches come in various shades and are ideal to patch up areas that have become worn. They come in lots of different sizes, too – tiny circles for holes or larger rectangular shapes you can cut to cover trickier areas. Machine washable and durable.

FIXING HOLES IN WOOLLENS

If you have caught a thread or moths have munched holes in your favourite sweater, don't throw it away as you can fix it with the use of bonding powder. By sprinkling on a little of this powder, you can repair tears, rips and holes in fabric. I only wish I'd known about this stuff before I lost several cashmere cardigans to moths. There are lots of fantastic books and YouTube videos showing how to repair your garments, so check those out first before you buy the bonding powder.

WATERPROOFING

Many raincoats, down coats or waterproof jackets start to let in water after a while. Rather than buying a new one, buy a re-proofing spray or wash. Look for water-based products which have the lowest impact on the environment. There are also re-proofing sprays available for leather, fabric and suede shoes, too.

REPURPOSE

Switch tired plastic buttons on cardigans, coats and jackets to ones made of wood, glass or natural shell. Add printed or stripy trims to sleeves, collars or hemlines to offer contrast to a plain t-shirt or dress. Attach ribbons and tassels to tops or jackets to create a bohemian feel. Embroider flowers onto pockets, hats, lapels and sneakers.

NATURAL DYING

White or light cotton t-shirts, dresses, shirts and skirts can be given a new lease of life simply by changing their colour. Coffee and tea make brown, onion skins make yellow, nettles make green, eucalyptus makes orange and avocados dye fabric a beautiful blush pink shade. Search online for tutorials on how to do this or borrow a book on natural dying from the library.

Create a capsule wardrobe

A capsule wardrobe is simply an edited version of what's already in your closet. You let go of the pieces that don't work and you keep the items you love: those clothes that make you feel great and fit well.

Having a capsule wardrobe frees you from the stress of deciding what to wear each morning, stops you from spending money on clothing you'll never wear, cuts down on clutter and allows you to become a more mindful consumer.

CHALLENGING YOURSELF TO ONLY WEAR CERTAIN ITEMS CAN HELP YOU TO FIND YOUR REAL STYLE AS YOU'LL DISCOVER WHAT SUITS YOU AND MAKES YOU FEEL MORE CONFIDENT.

If you have already decluttered your wardrobe (see pages 110–111), look at the items you have chosen to keep and ask yourself the following questions:

» Which colours do I mostly wear?
» What shapes or cut do I like best?
» Which materials work for me?
» Which store or brand works best for me?

These are your key pieces and the items you should base your capsule wardrobe around. The aim is to work these pieces hard by combining them in different ways to make several different outfits.

When the season changes, it's good to be able to pull a few things out of storage and make those the centre of your capsule wardrobe, storing the off-season pieces safely away from potential moth problems (see pages 112–113).

After you have pared back your closet to your favourite items, you'll discover what is missing. You may have lots of tops, shirts or t-shirts but only one or two skirts or pairs of trousers (pants).

Balancing out tops with bottoms will give you a flexible number of outfit combinations. If you need to buy something, look again at your answers to the questions above – which material, shape, cut or brand works best for you? Make slow and intentional purchases to fill the gaps.

Mindful shopping

I was once a terrible hoarder of fast fashion. I'd buy and buy, adding to the mountain of clothes that didn't fit in my closet or chest of drawers. Yet I still believed I had nothing to wear. Now I'm more mindful about what I choose to buy and I only shop for what I genuinely need. I've realized over the years that personal style isn't about wearing all the latest trends or copying a celebrity – it's about dressing in clothes that make me happy, that feel great and I can wear repeatedly without tiring of them.

Reducing your consumption of fast fashion can be tricky as it's a way many of us fill time, relieve boredom or to cheer ourselves up.

Here are some ways to help:

HOW TO CURB THE URGE

Create a secret Pinterest board for any potential fashion buys. If you are browsing online and you have the urge to put it in the shopping basket, stop and instead Pin it to your secret board. Leave it for a few days, return to the board and see if you still feel the urge to purchase. Chances are, you probably don't like it as much and you can let it go. Do the same for any sale items and if it is sold out by the time you go back to buy it, ask yourself, did you really miss out? The answer is usually no. This is one of the most effective ways I've found to stop myself purchasing unnecessary items over the years and I still use it today.

WINE MADE ME DO IT

Drinking and online shopping simply do not mix. It's a very easy thing to do and something many of us are guilty of. I've bought all kinds of stupid things to wear when I've been enjoying a glass or two! Hats, dresses, clogs with high heels – all things I never, ever wear but do admire on others. The mantra is an easy one to remember – don't drink and shop!

BUYING ON YOUR LUNCH BREAK

If you have time during your lunch hour to browse the stores, then choose to take your lunch outside instead. If it's a nice day, there could be a park, a bench with a nice view of the river or a shady spot under a tree to simply sit and enjoy the world going by. If it's wet or cold, perhaps there is a museum or an art gallery you could visit instead of hitting the stores. Search for local locations on Instagram and you may just discover some hidden gems, like a piece of street art, a secret garden or a new coffee shop. Look for drop-in activities like yoga, meditation or a drawing class where you could learn something new.

BUYING WITH INTENTION

When you go shopping for clothes, before you begin, consider a few practicalities:

» How do you spend your time – are you at home with the kids, do you work, walk the dog, play sports or socialize a lot? Your capsule wardrobe (see page 116) needs to reflect these activities.

» It's also useful to think about your location – does it rain a lot, is humidity a problem or do you have heavy snowfall and high winds to contend with? You'll need clothing that works for these conditions.

» If you need a more professional look, aim for two separate mini capsule collections – one for home, one for the workplace. Some items may be crossover ones, eg. a simple white shirt looks great with jeans or a black skirt.

Buy less, buy better

It's great to reduce your consumption of fast fashion and prioritize quality over quantity. I like to buy clothes that make me feel great, that fit my lifestyle and work with everything else in my wardrobe. I care about who makes my clothes and whether a company has a sound ethical policy regarding their staff and the environment.

I also want something that is made to last. Often these items cost a little more and I'm not going to lie and say that hasn't sometimes put me off buying them. Yet the key is to think about how much an item costs whilst weighing up how often you wear it. I've bought cheap jeans from a fast-fashion chain and I've bought more expensive organic cotton jeans. The expensive pair have been worn at least twice a week for three years and they still look great. The cheaper pair didn't even last a year.

In the same time span, I've spent less money on that one good pair than I would have buying several cheap pairs.

Here are some other ways to buy better and save you money:

BUY HANDMADE

You might think this sounds expensive and once upon a time I would have agreed with you. However, I've bought several linen tops and a pair of trousers (pants) that were handmade, and they were better quality and cheaper to buy than comparable ones on the high street. You have to wait a few weeks for your item to be made and be delivered, so order well in advance of when you may want to wear it. Search using hashtags on Instagram for handmade clothing or look on Etsy.

REPAIR YOUR GARMENT

There are several manufacturers out there who will offer to repair your item if it gets damaged. From backpacks and outdoor gear to boot makers, search online for companies that offer this additional service. Some will even take products back at the end of their lifespan and recycle them to make new goods.

LOOK FOR MAKERS WHO DO ONE THING WELL

These could be jeans, knitwear or t-shirt brands. These smaller companies often have strong ethical policies about where their raw materials comes from, they usually make everything in-house and they consider the impact their production methods have on the environment. And the product reflects how much they care about it.

CHILDREN'S CLOTHING

If you are a parent, you'll know how quickly babies and children get through clothing and many of us often resort to buying cheap clothing from supermarkets or chain stores. If you have several children, buying a few good-quality basics that can be handed down to siblings, friends or other family members is a great way to save money long-term. Look for plain t-shirts, hoodies, sweaters and coats.

Natural plant fibres

Natural fibres that are derived from plants are sustainable as they can be grown and harvested repeatedly. Clothing made from plant fibres is biodegradable and kinder to your skin. It's also a good investment as garments last longer, they don't pill and they tend to keep their shape better if you look after them properly.

When buying something new, look for clothing made from these natural plant fibres:

LINEN

Strong, durable and gets softer the more you wear it. Made from the flax plant, which can grow in poor soil, uses a lot less water than cotton and requires little to no pesticide. It doesn't require any chemicals to process it into fabric, is biodegradable and recyclable. Linen keeps you warm in cold weather and cool in hot temperatures. Look for linen clothing made in Europe as they have a strong environmental policy in place for growing and manufacturing. Search online for handmade linen dresses, jackets and tops. I have several items made from linen and I wouldn't be without them in my wardrobe.

HEMP

Like linen, hemp gets softer the more you wear it. It's three times more durable than cotton, keeps you warm in winter and cool in summer, resists mould and mildew and is naturally UV resistant. Hemp is fast-growing, uses little water and requires no pesticides. It also absorbs more carbon dioxide than trees. Nothing is wasted in the production of hemp; the seeds are used to make oil and the stalks are used for clothing fibres. It is often blended with organic cotton and you can find a wide range of fashion items for adults and kids made from the hemp plant.

ORGANIC COTTON

Conventional cotton is now the most pesticide-dependent crop in the world. These pesticides have been linked to surface and ground water contamination and drinking water pollution, and have caused irreparable harm to fish and wildlife. Switching to organic cotton helps to combat many of these problems as it uses far less water, requires no pesticides and increases biodiversity. Clothes made from organic cotton are gentler on the skin as the fibres are left intact and not broken down by the chemicals used in the farming and manufacturing of conventional cotton. Look for organic cotton denim, t-shirts, trainers (sneakers), trousers (pants), dresses and underwear.

LOOK OUT FOR

Brands that use GOTS-certified textiles (global organic textile standard). This certification means that the manufacturers use plants grown organically, use less energy and water, have less greenhouse gas emissions, treat their workers fairly, and their production methods are ecologically and socially responsible.

Vintage and second-hand clothing

VINTAGE AND SECOND-HAND SHOPPING IS ONE OF THE MOST SUSTAINABLE WAYS TO BUY CLOTHES.

You are helping to recycle garments that would otherwise end up in landfill as well as reducing the amount of resources needed to ship clothes to fashion outlets. Vintage pieces are unique, cheaper, and offer you a slice of social history, too.

If you have never bought vintage clothing and feel a little nervous about where to start, take the pressure off yourself by choosing accessories – a hat, a bag or a scarf are great ways to start. I began this way, bagging myself a beautiful tartan scarf and a basket bag that I knew no-one else had and they cost very little.

I like to source sweaters and cardigans from vintage shops or fairs as I know that I can find good woollen knitted ones, often made by hand and in my price range. Denim is a good buy as it gets softer the more it is worn and as one pair of new jeans uses over 10,000 litres of water during its manufacture, it's a greener choice to opt for the vintage pair. Woollen coats are good investment pieces to seek out, too.

VINTAGE STORES
Get to know the owners as they will help you to find what you are looking for, advise on fit and even source items if they know you are looking for something specific. I like to seek out stores when I visit other cities too.

CHARITY/THRIFT SHOPS

It's worth having a quick trip to your local charity shop or thrift store and seeing what stock they have, but my best tip is to head to the ones in more upmarket towns and cities as you tend to find better-quality garments.

ONLINE VINTAGE CLOTHING

If you are looking at vintage clothing on an online marketplace, it pays to be organized. Have a list of what you need as there are so many items listed that it's easy to miss the very thing you are looking for! It's essential to have a list of your measurements so you can work out if an item will fit. Measure your bust, waist and hips and add a little extra so that clothing is not skin tight. A lot of vintage clothing was tailored and cut in the style of that era so it's important to take this into account.

KILO SALES

Search online for your nearest event. Choose your items, weigh them and pay a pre-determined rate per kilo. One kilo will usually get you one outfit – a pair of jeans and a sweater or a dress, a bag and a pair of shoes. Stallholders replenish stock throughout the day, so it's worth popping in and out several times if you can.

CLOTHES SWAPPING EVENTS

You bring along a specific number of clean, good-quality pieces of clothing you no longer wear and swap them for the same number of items that others have brought. Search online for local events or set up your own swapping party with friends or colleagues.

Natural
Beauty

'Beauty awakens the soul to act.'
Dante Alighieri

Natural beauty

How many times have you added a bottle of shower gel, shampoo or body lotion to your basket and not given a second thought as to what is in it? I've done it so many times, never once glancing at the ingredients list. Yet, if we all took a little more care over what we put on our skin or reduced the number of products we buy, we could really make some positive changes.

Beauty is a very personal issue and it can be both emotionally and physically challenging for some.

From skin conditions and allergies to acne, there are many of us struggling to find the right balance between wellbeing and caring for the environment. If you have found a product that doesn't have the greatest green credentials but works for you, then don't change it. Instead, make a difference in other ways – buy a bamboo hair brush or swap disposable cotton wool balls to reusable cotton pads. It's always important to remember that sustainability must be sustainable to you.

Body care

Being more mindful of how we use water is vital. Switching to short showers instead of baths can save gallons of water. If it takes time for the water in your shower to heat up, pop a bucket underneath the flow and use that water for cleaning or watering plants. Unless you have kids, make baths an occasional treat and share the water with other members of your household where you can.

Try making some of these easy changes to your body care regime:

IN THE SHOWER

Switch from disposable plastic bottles of shower gel to a long-lasting bar of natural soap. My first choice is castile soap (see page 54) as it is great for moisturizing and can be used in so many ways – for hair, face and body. I also like to buy unpackaged bars of soap scented with essential oils from my local health food shop.

SOAP SAVER BAG

Buy a mesh soap saver bag made from bamboo. Pop your soap bar in the bag, wet the bag and then use it as a scrub. Any broken bits of soap are contained, and nothing is wasted. Hang it on a hook above the shower or bath to dry in between uses.

IN THE BATH

Choose natural zero-waste options like bath bombs or bubble bars, or make your own. Put a handful of oats inside a muslin square, add a few dried lavender flowers or rose petals and tie in place over the running water. For kids and babies, look for bubble baths free from parabens, sulfates, phthalates, synthetic colours and fragrances.

SHAVING EQUIPMENT

Switch from disposables plastics to a safety razor. Although it's more expensive to buy upfront and the blades are extra, it will save you money. The head of the razor doesn't move, it's heavier to hold and it takes a bit of practice to get a close shave, but it fits all blades, so if you have a preferred brand, you can use them. The handle can last a lifetime if looked after properly. Visit a professional barber or shaving store as they will help you choose the right razor.

RAZOR BLADE SHARPENER

Cleans off any microscopic residue and sharpens the blade from any razor, including disposables (for men and women). Using one of these can make your blades last up to six times longer and reduce the numbers of disposables bought and thrown away.

SHAVING CREAM/SOAP

Switch from tubes or canisters of shaving gel to a natural shaving cream or soap. Creams are soft and can often be applied directly to a shaving brush, while firmer soaps need to be mixed with a little warm water to create a lather. After shaving, apply a natural balm made from soothing coconut oil, sweet almond oil and vitamin E.

continued »

WAXING

For hair removal, the eco choice is a natural sugar wax. Made from sugar, essential oils and vegetable glycerine, it is suitable for sensitive skin and is vegan. Look for products made with organic ingredients, packaged in glass jars and that come with reusable spatulas and washable paper strips. Alternatively, you can make your own sugar wax at home – look online for tutorials.

BEARD OIL

Look for products that use natural oils, such as olive, argan, sweet almond or vitamin E, to help moisturize and nourish. Avoid brands using artificial fragrances and choose small-batch oils that are scented with essential oils.

SCRUBS

Making your own exfoliating scrub is easy and it's a great feeling to step into the shower with something you have created yourself. I like to use lemon and lavender oils in my homemade scrub which makes it smell incredible, but you could switch to other essential oils if you prefer. I've recommended using five to ten drops of each oil, but feel free to add a few more drops if you like a stronger scent.

The recipe opposite also uses the zest of one lemon and a few dried lavender flowers, which are purely for decoration and are not essential.

This scrub makes the perfect low-waste gift for Christmas and birthdays or a thank you for teachers. Use a recycled jam jar, fill with the scrub, add a small sprig of lavender on top for a pretty touch, seal and decorate with a brown paper tag listing the ingredients.

How to make sea salt scrub with lemon and lavender

MAKES 1 JAR

» 125g (½ cup) coarse sea salt
» 80ml (5½ tablespoons) sweet almond oil
» 5–10 drops of lavender essential oil
» 5–10 drops of lemon essential oil
» Zest of 1 unwaxed lemon (optional)
» A few dried lavender flowers (optional)
» 1 clean jar with a lid

1 Mix the sea salt with the almond oil in a bowl.

2 Add the essential oils and mix again. Stir through the lemon zest and the dried lavender flowers (if using). Transfer to a clean jar and seal.

TO USE

Once your skin is wet all over, pop a little of the scrub on your fingertips and gently rub your skin in circular motions to remove any dead skin cells. Rinse off and gently pat dry with a towel. Regular exfoliation leaves your skin feeling softer and smoother – I like to use a sea salt scrub once a week.

Use within 1 month of making.

Natural skincare

Adopting simple changes to your skincare routine can be hugely beneficial to the environment – waste is significantly reduced, less non-renewables are required, and no harmful chemicals are released into the water supply. Try some of these ideas:

COTTON WOOL
Switch from cotton wool balls or pads to reusable cotton/hemp pads for removing make-up. They can go in the washing machine on a low temperature or you can give them a quick handwash with some liquid castile soap (see page 54). If you choose to add them to your washing machine, pop them in a washable drawstring bag to stop them getting lost amongst the rest of the laundry. When they come to the end of their life add your biodegradable pads into the compost

KONJAC SPONGE
Derived from the konjac potato plant, this is a natural fibre rich in minerals. Konjac sponges are sustainable, vegan, non-toxic and very gentle on the skin. You simply soak the sponge in warm water until it expands, then use with or without cleanser. Rinse the sponge in cold water after use, gently squeeze and hang it up to air dry. You can buy natural sponges or ones with added mineral powders, such as bamboo charcoal to help acne sufferers and green clay for oily skin. Good for skin conditions like eczema, psoriasis and rosacea. Sterilize in boiling water once every 2 weeks and each sponge should last for 4–6 weeks. They are also biodegradable and compostable.

BEAUTY WIPES
Instead of reaching for conventional brands which contain plastic, switch to a pack

of organic cotton wipes which are biodegradable and compostable. Perfect for camping trips or if you have no access to clean water, but it's important not to rely on them for everyday use. Never flush wipes down the toilet.

BEAUTY BALM

The ultimate multi-tasking product. Use it with a hot muslin or bamboo cloth as a cleanser. It's also a moisturizer, hand cream, lip balm, facial mask, foot cream, sun-burn soother, scar treatment and a soothing cream for bug bites. Look for products with all-natural ingredients that come in recyclable glass jars. If you are vegan, be sure to check that your chosen balm doesn't contain beeswax.

FACIAL OIL

Perfect to use after your cleansing routine, facial oils are made with plant extracts such as rosehip seed or argan oil. They hydrate, smoothen and make your skin glow. They are suitable for all skin types and are best used overnight. Facial oils are also great for city dwellers as they provide extra protection against pollution. Buy products in recyclable glass bottles.

LIP BALM

Most conventional products contain petroleum jelly, a by-product of the oil industry, and many contain synthetic fragrances, parabens and mineral oils too. Look for alternatives made from beeswax, shea butter or coconut oil, packaged in small tins that can be easily recycled. As well as avoiding beeswax, vegans also need to be aware that lanolin – a product commonly used in lip balm – is derived from sheep, so double check the ingredients before you buy.

EYE CARE

Try this natural fix to ease tired eyes and help combat dark circles. Soak a reusable pad in cold chamomile tea. Squeeze out excess liquid, then apply to the eyes and leave for 10 minutes.

Cosmetics

The natural cosmetic industry is going through a period of rapid growth and it has never been easier to switch to products that use plant-derived ingredients and less plastic packaging. With an enormous array of green beauty products to choose from, it's important to do a little research to ensure a brand's eco credentials are honest. Good companies will tell you on their websites how they started, what their mission is and which ingredients they use, and they will also be happy to answer questions from customers. A great brand will also be willing to let you take home or send out samples of certain products, so you can try before you buy.

If you still have some conventional products left, use them up first before you switch to an eco-alternative. Many cosmetics can be recycled too – glass bottles, plastics and aerosols can usually be collected kerbside. Some brands offer recycling programmes of their own where you return empty containers and receive a discount or a free product in return.

Change one product at a time as this allows your skin to adapt gently and gradually, and it will be easier on your budget, too. Read reviews on cosmetics posted by natural beauty bloggers who have a similar skin type or colouring to you as this can also be beneficial in discovering new and established brands. Look for products that carry the 'suitable for vegans' label as that means they are free from animal testing and no animal-derived ingredients are in the formula.

FACE & EYES

Switch to products made with plant-derived and organic ingredients. Avoid synthetic dyes and choose colours that come from fruit and vegetable pigments. Some natural beauty brands now offer refillable options for foundation, blusher, mascara, eye shadows and pencils, which save on packaging and money too.

LIPSTICK

Big beauty brand lipsticks contain synthetic chemicals that do harm to the environment and are often tested on animals. Make a simple switch to lipsticks made from natural beeswax or for vegans, look for products that contain candelilla wax and coconut oil.

MAKE-UP REMOVAL PADS

Rather than purchasing single use facial wipes or cotton balls, switch to reusable organic cotton pads. You simply wet the pad, take off your make-up, rinse with cold water and leave to dry. You can use each pad several times before adding them to the laundry for a deeper clean.

NAIL POLISH

One of the biggest offenders in the beauty industry is nail polish as it is full of toxic chemicals. However, brands are starting to clean up their act and have removed certain nasties from their ingredients including formaldehyde, dibutyl phthalate, triphenyl phosphate, parabens and camphor. Check the label before you buy to see if it lists the number of toxins removed – it's usually on a scale of '3-free-to-10-free'. The higher the number, the more eco the polish.

NAIL POLISH REMOVER

Switch to acetone-free, non-toxic, biodegradable soy nail polish remover. Choose unscented products which are odourless and safe for use by pregnant women, nursing mothers and kids.

Natural haircare

Your hair is essentially addicted to the chemicals found in the commercial products many of us use, so when you make the change to natural products your hair will have withdrawal symptoms. Switching to a natural product is like putting your hair through a detox, one that will make it look and feel unhappy at first. However, stick with it and your scalp and the environment will thank you in the long term.

NATURAL SHAMPOO

Look for brands that are free from parabens, phthalates and sulfates. Choose naturally derived ingredients and fragrances made from real plants, herbs or fruits. You may need to try a few different brands until you find one that works for you. For best results, shampoo, then rinse well, shampoo a second time and rinse again. You may find your scalp is itchy, and your hair is heavy and more oily than normal for the first few days. After a few washes, your hair and scalp will adapt and become shinier and healthier.

SHAMPOO BARS

A good zero-waste option, especially if you buy them unpackaged. Be aware that some do contain SLS, a sulfate that is used to make the bar lather up, while others are made purely from natural oils and scented with essential oils. It may take several attempts to find a bar that works well for you and, much like switching to a natural shampoo, your scalp will need time to adjust.

APPLE CIDER VINEGAR RINSE

Works as a natural detangler, removes product build-up, adds shine and reduces frizz. It's antibacterial and antifungal, too. Buy ready-made rinses or look for online tutorials on how to make your own with herbs and essential oils.

'NO POO' METHOD

Frequent washing with conventional shampoo can strip away the natural oils in your hair, making it too dry or too greasy, and you end up reaching for other products to combat these issues. With the 'no poo' method, the idea is to allow your hair to return to its natural balanced state. You wash your hair with water only or 1 tablespoon bicarbonate of soda (baking soda) dissolved in a glass of water which you lather into your scalp before rinsing. Switching to the 'no poo' method can smell unpleasant during this adjustment period, but after a couple of weeks the smell disappears, and hair is left shiny and clean.

HAIR COLOURANTS

Conventional hair colouring products are made with ammonia, a chemical that has been linked to skin and eye irritation as well as respiratory problems. They also contain PPD and PTD, two ingredients that are derived from petroleum. If you regularly visit the salon to have your hair coloured, look online for organic hair salons where experts use natural colouring treatments. Alternatively, you can buy natural hair colourants to use at home. Most come in a powder form, others as a henna bar, and they are mixed with warm water to form a paste that you apply to your hair. However, grey coverage can be patchy.

Deodorants

We all sweat, and it can be a major cause of embarrassment for some. It's a problem I struggled with in the past and I had to buy anti-perspirants of the more industrial variety to try and keep it under control.

Sweat is your body's natural way of cooling down, and we tend to produce more when we are under stress, feeling nervous or we've been exercising. The bad odour is created when sweat meets the natural bacteria that live on our skin. Of course, this makes us automatically reach for anti-perspirants and deodorants that promise us freedom from

unpleasant aroma and wet armpits. These products work by temporarily blocking the pores to prevent the body from sweating and typically contain some nasty ingredients – aluminium, phthalates, propylene glycol and parabens. Spray versions also release potentially harmful VOCs (see page 19), which significantly contribute to indoor air pollution.

Switching to a natural deodorant is the answer – no nasty chemicals are used, and no harmful VOCs are released into the air. However, many people struggle to find the right product that works for them, and it can take several attempts until you find one that does. I tried a few before I finally found one that suited me. The key is to keep testing and don't give up! It's important to apply natural deodorants to clean, dry armpits and to let any product dry thoroughly before you get dressed.

There are various types of natural deodorant available – sticks, sprays and creams. As the sticks are always packaged in plastic, I prefer sprays or creams as they come in recyclable glass bottles and pots. Buy samples first to test them out before you invest in a bigger size.

ARMPIT DETOX

Before you start using a natural deodorant, it's a good idea to give your body a little time to adjust from the previous products you have used. Doing a weekend detox is best – apply your commercial product as usual on Friday morning, then use nothing through Saturday and Sunday before applying the new natural deodorant on Monday morning. Be warned – there is a good chance you will smell bad during the detox. Drink plenty of water and exfoliate your armpits in the shower using a sea salt scrub (see page 133).

CREAM

Usually made with coconut oil, shea butter, essential oils and bicarbonate of soda (baking soda) as the main ingredients. If you have very sensitive skin, you may find you have an allergy to the bicarbonate of soda, so look for brands that are baking soda-free. To apply, put a tiny amount onto your fingertips and lightly wipe it into your armpits.

SPRAY

Usually alcohol-based and scented with essential oils. This will sting a little when you first apply it, especially after you have shaved. Be aware that some brands include tallow as an ingredient, which means they are not suitable for vegans.

Dentalcare

I suffer from sensitive teeth, so need to use a toothpaste that helps keep that under control. Sadly, it's a cheap, supermarket own brand that works best for me and it comes in a plastic tube. Not ideal, I know, but I try to compensate for this by using other sustainable dental products.

TOOTHBRUSHES

Billions of plastic toothbrushes and their packaging head to landfill every year and as they are not biodegradable, they will simply sit there for hundreds of years. Try switching to toothbrushes with handles made from bamboo as these are biodegradable and compostable if you first remove the nylon bristles. Bamboo is strong, flexible and naturally resistant to bacteria. You need to keep them dry as bamboo will turn black if left to sit in water, so give them a quick wipe down with a towel after use and store in a clean, dry

cup. It felt like I was putting a bit of tree bark in my mouth the first few times I used one, but it soon passes! You can find them in all sizes, including kids' brushes.

NATURAL TOOTHPASTE AND TOOTHPOWDER

Many natural toothpaste brands have chosen to remove fluoride from their products and it is the subject of much debate over its benefits in preventing tooth decay. Conventional brands also use triclosan in toothpaste and mouthwash, which is an antibacterial compound that has been linked to long-term health problems. It's a good idea to discuss switching to a natural toothpaste with your dentist before you commit. Natural products are usually made with bicarbonate of soda (baking soda) to polish, whiten and neutralize plaque acids. They are often flavoured with essential oils – peppermint, tea tree or spearmint, and you can also find kids' versions made in fruit flavours. There are lots of online on how tutorials to make your own, too.

DENTAL FLOSS
Dental floss is conventionally made from nylon, a petroleum-based plastic which comes in a pre-packaged disposable container. Both inevitably end up in landfill. Switch to silk floss, coated with beeswax which is biodegradable and compostable. There are alternatives made with nylon and coated with plant or vegetable wax

for vegans. Look for brands that also use compostable packaging or supply their floss in glass containers which can be refilled.

FLOSSING HARP/PICK
There are now versions of these that are fully biodegradable and compostable, or look for a reusable one and buy refill spools of floss.

MOUTHWASH
Switch from conventional bottles that contain triclosan and synthetic dyes to a natural mouthwash in tablet form. You pop a tab in your mouth, add a little water for it to fizz a little, gargle and spit. If you don't like the fizzing effect in your mouth, you can dissolve the tablet in a small glass of water instead. Look for brands that use glass bottles that can be recycled.

Personal care

The average woman using tampons or sanitary pads throws away over 11,000 during her lifetime. Cotton pads or tampons usually biodegrade within six months, but the plastic packaging, wraps and applicators can take years. Switching to planet-friendly alternatives has never been easier and there are lots of great options available.

MENSTRUAL CUP

The top eco choice as it can last for ten years and you won't have to use tampons or pads again. Once inserted, the cup can stay in place for as long as 12 hours, although it's best to change it every 4 – 8 hours. Made from medical-grade silicon, it is available in two sizes, depending on your flow. To use, you simply fold and insert, then remove, empty, rinse or wipe and then re-insert. Sterilize between periods by boiling in hot water or use a sterilizing solution or tablet.

PERIOD UNDERWEAR

Like regular underwear, but these have the added advantage of being fully absorbent, anti-bacterial and leakproof. Many women choose to go with their usual product for the first couple of days of their period, switching to these pants for lighter flow days, while others choose to wear them every day. There are lots of versions of these on the market – some with removable inserts that you change throughout the day, others with pouches that can conceal a heat pad. There are several design options – thong, boxer, bikini, etc, and you can find brands that use organic cotton, too. They are ideal if you have a heavy discharge, postpartum discharge or bladder leakage. Rinse with cold water, then pop them in a mesh bag, stick the bag in the washing machine and use an eco-friendly washing powder to clean. Line dry.

REUSABLE SANITARY PADS

Made from organic cotton or bamboo, these pads come in a variety of sizes to suit flow types, and extra protective layers for night-time wear. After use, rinse them in cold water, put them in a wash bag and once it's full, you can simply pop the bag and pads in the washing machine.

ORGANIC COTTON TAMPONS

Conventional tampons are made from a mixture of rayon and cotton, chlorine-bleached and then wrapped in plastic. Many come with plastic applicators too.

Switching to an organic cotton tampon is a good alternative as they are free from pesticides, dyes, chlorine and rayon. They are also hypoallergenic, biodegradable and compostable.

REUSABLE TAMPON APPLICATOR

Perfect if you prefer to use an applicator tampon but want to reduce the amount of waste you produce. This reusable version fits every size of tampon, is antimicrobial and easy to insert. After use, give it a quick wipe, rinse and return to the compact storage box that easily fits in your handbag. Sterilize in hot water between periods.

PREGNANCY TESTING

Commercial tests are made of plastic, wrapped in plastic packaging and ultimately end up in landfill. There is a greener alternative now on the market – a test that is made of paper and is fully flushable, biodegradable and compostable.

Simple Christmas

"Maybe Christmas", he thought,
"doesn't come from a store."
"Maybe Christmas...perhaps...
means a little bit more!"

Dr. Seuss, *How the Grinch*
Stole Christmas

Simple Christmas

There are many ways we can live more sustainably at Christmas. We can buy a little less, choose recycled paper Christmas cards or send e-cards instead of printed ones, reduce our use of wrapping paper and tape, or adopt a 'no Secret Santa' policy in the workplace and give money to charity instead.

Living simply and sustainably over the holidays doesn't take away any of the joy of Christmas. If anything, it's a lot better, as the pressures of endless shopping are removed, you learn to appreciate what you have, and you can relax in a home that is calmer and kinder to your family and the environment.

Christmas trees

Putting the Christmas tree up in December is always an occasion to be celebrated, and it's when the magic of the season really begins for many.

We bring our tree into the house on the first Saturday of December and decorate it simply with white fairy lights, a few treasured baubles, a garland of dried citrus slices (see page 152) and a homemade paper star at the top of the tree. For me, the best thing is the smell of a real tree, as it scents my home with the heady aromas of citrus and pine.

How do you decide which kind of tree is the most sustainable option? If you buy a fake plastic tree, it will last for a long time. However, when it begins to look shabby, it will need to be replaced and will ultimately end up in landfill where it will take hundreds of years to breakdown. If you choose a real cut tree, it is only used for a few weeks before being thrown out with the garden waste and recycled.

These are the best ethical and sustainable options:

CUT TREE FROM LOCAL FARM

Rather than buying from a garden centre, hardware chain or supermarket, look for a local farm that grows their own trees. Christmas trees take years to grow, and for every tree cut down, there will be several more planted in its place. Ask questions about how the trees are grown, looked after and felled. Many will let you go into the field and pick your own tree before cutting it down in front of you. Supporting local businesses benefits your community and cuts down on transport too.

POT TREE

This is either a tree that has been grown in a container or one that has been dug up with its roots intact and put in a container filled with potting compost. They are kept indoors over the holiday period, then placed outside in the garden until the following year. This is ideal for smaller spaces, but the tree will need repotting into a larger container every couple of years to ensure it stays healthy and you need to remember to water it well during dry spells. You can then bring the tree and container back into your home the following Christmas.

HOW TO LOOK AFTER YOUR CHRISTMAS TREE

If you buy a tree that was possibly felled a while ago, treat it like a bunch of flowers. Saw a little off the trunk to allow the tree to absorb water (you don't need to do this if you have bought a freshly cut tree). Position well away from radiators as this can dry them out. Make sure the base of the trunk is always in a bowl of fresh water, but look out for curious dogs and cats. Sweep up any needles with a dustpan and brush, then add them to your compost bin.

REUSABLE CARDBOARD/ WOOD TREE

The ultimate choice for sustainability. You can find companies who sell these, but they are relatively easy to make yourself using recycled materials. Look online where you'll find some great tutorials for contemporary shapes, bold geometrics and minimalist designs.

Christmas decorations

I like to keep decorations simple and natural at Christmas. My favourite way to embrace the holiday is to go on a foraging walk and gather twigs, pine cones, evergreens and berries. Along with candlelight and a few twinkling fairy lights, my home is cosy and festive.

WREATHS

Make your own rustic wreath with a reusable brass or copper ring as the base. Add sprigs of evergreens, Christmas tree branch trimmings, berries, bay leaves, olive branches, pine cones and eucalyptus.

DRIED CITRUS GARLAND

Slice oranges into 1-cm (½-in) widths. Cut a small hole in the top of each slice so you can thread it later. Set your oven to the lowest temperature. Arrange the slices on a baking sheet lined with baking paper and bake for 4 hours. When the slices have cooled, string them onto some jute twine. They look beautiful draped around the tree or hanging across the mantelpiece.

SCENTED PINE CONES

Soak the pine cones in cold water, rinse, then place them on a baking sheet lined with foil. Pop in the oven at 180°C/350°F/Gas 4 and bake for around 30–60 minutes. Keep an eye on them to make sure they don't burn. Remove from the oven and allow to cool. Place them in a large sealable bag and add a few drops of essential oils – cloves, cinnamon, nutmeg, orange or pine all work well. Seal the bag, then shake and leave for several days. Add more oils if you need a stronger scent. Display in a wooden bowl or make a rustic garland of pine cones strung on natural twine.

CANDLES

I use tealights and scented candles made with rapeseed (canola), beeswax or soy wax (see page 32). Dinner candles made in a sustainable way are far harder to find, but they are available in some stores and, of course, online.

» Pop a tealight in a glass holder and line the rim with sprigs of evergreen rosemary. Attach with some jute twine tied in a small bow. Recycled jam jars work well for this project.

» Use tiny vintage terracotta pots or vintage cups as candle holders.

» Recycle clear glass wine or cordial bottles. Wash and remove the labels. Boil the kettle, allow the water to cool, then fill the bottles about two-thirds full. Add a sprig of greenery to each bottle – fresh herbs like thyme or rosemary or eucalyptus all look stunning displayed this way. Using boiled water helps to stop discolouration occurring in the bottle.

TABLE SETTINGS

At each place setting, roll up a napkin and tie a length of jute twine around it, with the bow pointing upwards. Tuck some natural elements into the twine – try a sprig of mistletoe or rosemary, a cinnamon stick, a dried orange slice, a sprig of rosehips or a tiny scented pine cone.

Gift ideas

I love Christmas – the smells, the food, movies both good and bad, and most of all being with my family. What I really don't like is the overconsumption, buying things we don't really like or need, the enormous amount of waste and the greed of so many. Adopting a more ethical approach means shopping is more enjoyable and we can gift something truly unique to the people we care about.

DONATE TO OR JOIN A CHARITABLE PROJECT

Buy a membership of an environmental charity or an animal welfare charity. Donate to local charitable initiatives – conservation projects, community gardens or a nature reserve.

CHOOSE EXPERIENCES OVER MATERIAL GOODS

Buy cinema or theatre tickets, or a restaurant voucher for a family meal. Book places on a workshop to learn a new skill – calligraphy, photography, bread making, preserve making, foraging, ceramics or weaving.

MAKE YOUR OWN BEAUTY PRODUCTS

Rather than buy commercial gift packs of body lotion and bubble bath, have a go at making your own. Look online for tutorials to make your own bath oils or try the recipe on page 133 for an exfoliating salt scrub scented with lavender and lemon. Gather flowers and herbs throughout the summer months to give them time to dry out. Rose petals, lavender stems, calendula, chamomile and eucalyptus all work well for this.

PERSONAL VOUCHER

Offer up a service to a family member or friend. It could be an evening of babysitting, helping them in the garden or serving breakfast in bed.

EDIBLES

Put together hampers of local products, such as cheeses, crackers, preserves, chutney and honey. Or better still, make your own – cookies, cakes, jams, cordials or bottles of sloe gin (see page 95) make fantastic gifts.

GROW

I like to give wildflower seed bombs, fruit trees or houseplants as gifts. I also put together packets of seeds linked to an interest or hobby and tie them with jute twine. Add a simple sprig of dried lavender or rosemary for decoration.

» *Herbal tea fans* Go for chamomile, fennel, lemon balm and peppermint. For an extra touch, arrange the sachets in a vintage teacup.

» *Italian cooking* Choose basil, marjoram, oregano and thyme seeds, and add a nice glass bottle of olive oil.

» *Cocktails* Borage, hyssop, lemon balm, mint. Look for vintage cocktail shakers or glasses for added glamour.

GIVE LESS

One of the simplest ways to be greener is to not buy lots of extras. If your child has asked for one specific toy, that's what they are really looking for, not lots of cheap plastic items that will be relegated to the bottom of the toybox. Choose one or two additional toys that will be played with and add in other more useful items like clothing, books or vouchers.

REGIFTING

This works particularly well with kids' presents, accessories or beauty gift sets. If it's a duplicate or is not going to be used and is still in good condition, regift it (although it's best not to give it back to the person who bought it originally!).

Gift wrapping

Every year I used to get a little downhearted at how much rubbish we created from gift giving. From the wrapping paper packaged in plastic, gift tags and sticky tape to the single-use plastic-coated gift bags, it all ultimately ended up in landfill. And it's the same for most households.

Now I wrap gifts with fabric using the Japanese technique, furoshiki. It's reusable, creates no waste and it's also far more pleasant spending an afternoon folding and tying than dealing with scissors, paper and tape.

I like to use pieces of cotton and linen fabric as the cloth is strong enough to support a little weight and as it's opaque, no one can see what's inside the parcel. Pieces of fabric cut from old clothing or bedlinen also work well or seek out vintage fabrics, dish towels and silk scarves for something a little bit different.